M000200991

Following on
SEAS of GLORY

Adventures at Sea and Around the World

LEONARD H. GAFFGA LCDR USNR (RET.)

© 2020 by Leonard H. Gaffga

ISBN: 978-1-54399-936-5

Printed in the United States of America

First Edition

All rights reserved. No part of this book may be reproduced, scanned, or distributed in any printed or electronic form without permission. Please do not participate in or encourage piracy of copyrighted materials in violation of the author's rights. Purchase only authorized editions.

gaffga@hargray.com

DEDICATION

to my father
Leonard Ward Gaffga
1905–1993

CONTENTS

PREFACE

My earliest exposure to the power and tradition of the U.S. Navy was as a youngster watching *Victory at Sea* on Saturday mornings on TV. The great warships, the sea battles, and the victories we won, stuck in my mind. As I grew older these maritime images were enlarged and augmented by the heroics (not always verbalized) of real-life relatives who had gone to sea. Their experiences combined the dangers of a powerful and unpredictable sea with the dangers of mortal combat. Thus, as a youngster, my image of a wider world and the boundless oceans beyond took shape. And like so many of my contemporaries, I was pressed into service in a time of war. Many of us were deeply changed by our experiences.

Leaving Garden City, New York for Officer Candidate School (OCS) in Newport, Rhode Island.

Assisted by pictures, recollections, research, and some official documents from my experience in the U.S. Navy, I have assembled the following through which I hope describe some of the lessons I learned and the challenges I faced while serving my country mostly overseas and abroad.

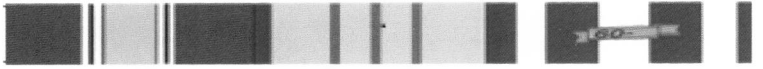

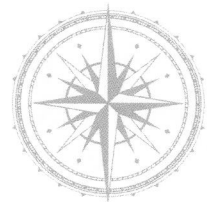

ACKNOWLEDGEMENTS

I am deeply grateful to my wife, Cathy, for encouraging me to keep up my pace in writing this book. It took longer than I expected, and I felt her support kicking in as we neared the finish line. Her support has meant so much to me over the years as I related the events of what was probably the most important time of my life. She has never failed to cherish every detail of my experience.

My three sons have always been interested in hearing my sea stories from the time they were young and long before I began to write them down. They were always excited to make the trip to Naval Station, Mayport and to go aboard a Navy ship. They were fascinated by the pictures I showed them, my uniform hanging in the closet and how I was able to join the Navy and see the world. I am grateful that they seemed to catch the excitement of my escapades.

When I arrived in Del Webb's Sun City Hilton Head in 2007 for the purpose of beginning retired life, I was greeted by a beehive of activity in the form of clubs and associations I could join. At first, most of it seemed like busy-work to me. The advice I got was all over the map.

But one person stands out for the advice he gave me. Almost like a mentor, Arnold Rosen said, "Do two things: write your military history and join the community theater". I did both. I even sang "Anchors, aweigh" at my tryout for a small singing part in Cole Porter's "Anything Goes".

But it was the encouragement I got from Arnold Rosen that kept me plodding along through several iterations and over several years that produced this book that you are now reading. The fact is that I never even knew I might like to write until I met Arnold. And then it seemed possible.

Through a stroke of good fortune, I was able to thank him in person for his advice before he passed. He too, was busy, writing at least three books on the personal stories - challenges and accomplishments - of our aging veterans.

CHAPTER 1

Down to the Sea as My Father before Me—A Final Tribute

L ong Island Sound, in the early days of June 1923, was still far enough away from the gathering heat and dust of New York City. Its shores were undeveloped, and they surrounded a body of water so beautiful as to invite all who would sail or swim. The school ship *SS Newport* lay at anchor in the middle of Hempstead Harbor, a white beauty, riding like a swan. A hundred boys were going through the drills and exercises intended to prepare them for that still greater voyage across a thousand leagues of the Atlantic itself.

New York State Merchant Marine Academy School Ship SS Newport

The exercises and the wholesome food and regular hours of sleep, with all hands out in the open air and sunshine, began to tell upon the entire cadet complement. They were like a picked group of athletes—handling sails, lowering and furling, with increasing facility. It was the beginning of the experience of a lifetime for my father, one of the cadets at the New York State Merchant Marine Academy.

My father was born in a sleepy, little fishing village 100 miles east of New York City in 1905 to a prominent family in Greenport, Long Island. I say "prominent" because my grandfather, John Schmidt Gaffga, was the inventor of a gasoline engine that he manufactured and sold for fishing boats and pleasure boats alike between 1901 and 1925. Naturally, my father, Leonard W. Gaffga (who was the youngest of three sons) grew up on the water and even had a small boat himself powered by a "Gaffga" marine engine. Note the name cast into the block on this four-cylinder model.

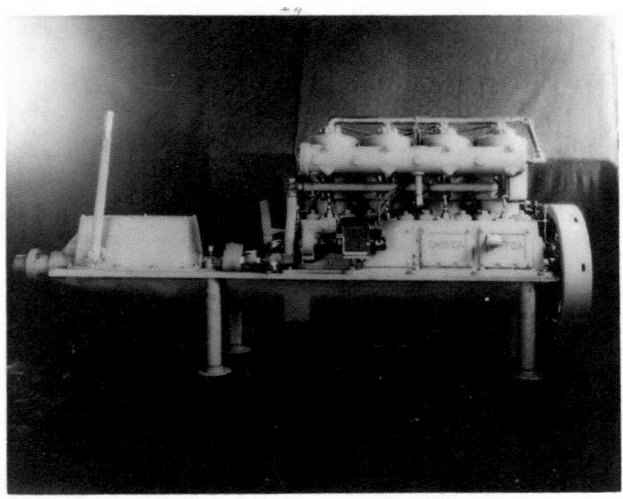

The Gaffga marine engine.

My father was a great storyteller and among the many he told my sister, Judy and me, was the story of how he saved the life of a cook that worked at one of the hotels on Shelter Island from drowning. The cook was trying to swim from Greenport across a narrow channel to Shelter Island. And, although it doesn't look like a great distance to swim, the current, which is swift and powerful at that point, is what almost did him in. My father happened to be out on the water that day and pulled the cook into his boat as the guy was being carried out to sea by the current.

Residence of John S. Gaffga, North Street
Village Trustee

My grandparents' home in Greenport, Long Island, New York.

Fishing and boating were normal activities for me growing up while on visits to my grandparents and my other relatives in Greenport. I often went fishing on the jetty with my Uncle Jack. When I was young, I would stay a week or so with my grandmother, Flora, in their very nice house on North Street in town and within walking distance of the waterfront. I can still picture my grandfather with his white hair, who died while I was still young. The waterfront, with its many docks, was my favorite place in town to explore. By the 1950s, there were more pleasure boats and fewer fishing boats because by then Greenport had morphed from a fishing village into a tourist destination. People from New York City were vacationing there in the summers. It was also an agricultural area famous in the 1950s for its Long Island Potatoes.

The 6:00 Whistle

Interior View of the Power Plant

The "light plant" in Greenport.

Around 5:30 every afternoon, I climbed on the bicycle that my grand-mother kept in the garage for me and would ride down a long dirt road to the "light plant," as it was called, where big diesel engines produced electricity for the village. I heard tell that my grandfather had a lot to do with getting those engines installed in at the plant. My Uncle Jack ran the light plant. The noise of those engines was deafening. At a few minutes before 6:00 pm, Uncle Jack would direct me to grab hold of the long rope that went clear up to the ceil-ing and, at his command, pull it with all my might (i.e., weight). I blew the 6:00 whistle for what seemed like an eternity. I blew it for every villager within earshot to hear, before my uncle would signal me to stop. It was kind of an industrial age equivalent of ringing church bells in a medieval town, which kept the town running on schedule. People didn't have wristwatches back then, and today we don't have 6:00 whistles. Then I'd ride home to have dinner with my grandmother.

My grandmother is pictured in the backyard with my mother, father, and me when I was about 10 or 11 years old below. She was a very kindly person and lived by herself on North Street until the age of 91.

My grandmother, my parents, and me when I was about 10 or 11 years old.

Uncle Walter, her oldest son, his wife Marjorie and my three cousins lived two doors down on North Street. Uncle Walter sailed on merchant ships to France during World War I (WWI) braving German U-boats and afterward he worked in Brigham's Shipyard for the remainder of his life. (See German U-boats in *Fall of Giants* by Ken Follett.) Young Walter, my cousin who was just a few years older than me, commuted by boat every day to his job on Plum Island. He worked in a government laboratory that developed vaccines to eradicate hoof and mouth disease.

My grandmother's middle son, *Uncle Jack* and his wife Jane Tillinghast had a son who was born in 1920; I never met him because he died in World War II (WWII) in Italy. Leonard Tillinghast Gaffga was a commodore of the local Power Squadron before joining the service. We were a family with strong ties to the sea.

Leonard W. Gaffga, her youngest son and his wife Ruth Hilkert lived in New York City where I was born. Their children are Leonard H. Gaffga (me) and Judy Acord (my sister).

My boyhood friends in Garden City, Long Island, New York.

The photo above is of my boyhood friends at Garden City High School. Two of them, Wade (extreme left) and Eric (extreme right) had summer places out on the end of the island. They had sailboats and I was invited by Wade to "crew" for him in a race. After the race, there were festivities at the yacht club; dinner, dancing, and socializing. Wade and I liked to listen to Joan Baez songs on the record player. Every morning, Wade and I walked over to the ice company near their home and brought home a *big block of ice for the ice box.*

Gene Shepherd and my father demonstrate the Gaffga marine engine.

A number of years ago, Cathy, my second wife, and I were back on Long Island for my High School Reunion (50th) and we drove out to see my grandfather's engine, which was on display in a museum on Shelter Island. The museum was run by Gene Shepherd. My father (right) is about 75 years old in this picture taken in 1980. Gene had two of the engines outside and running for us to see. It was a thrill to finally see and hear the Gaffga engine up close.

During our visit, I suggested that we knock on Wade's parents front door. I easily found Wade's house in Shelter Island Heights and knocked. A woman came to the door and when she saw who was there, she *immediately called my name*. I was so impressed with her memory. She invited us in, and Wade's father came down the stairs. We started talking about a boat he owned as a young boy on Shelter Island and especially about the Gaffga engine that powered it. What a surprise that he owned a Gaffga engine! But then he made a comment about the engine that I just as soon forget. He said, "That was the worst engine I ever owned!" *Now I was shocked!* What was his problem? To start the engine, you must turn the flywheel (red in the picture). And there is a handle built into the flywheel which is used to turn it—not a self-starting engine. When the engine catches, the flywheel will sometimes kick over and if you're not careful it can almost break your knuckles. It hurts. That is what Wade's father didn't like about it. Such is the stuff of a legacy.

Article in the Suffolk Times (July 15, 1943)

The Gaffga Motor Was Popular When Gasoline Was Plentiful
A reminder of the by-gone days when the marine gasoline motor was in its infancy and gasoline was plentiful was recalled to mind several days ago when former Village Trustee John S. Gaffga received a post card from Minnesota. Mr. Gaffga, who was one of the pioneers in the field of marine gasoline motors, established the Gaffga Marine Motor Company in 1901 and continued in business until 1925 when he sold the business." (Author Note: By 1943, during WWII, gasoline was very scarce.)

During the years that the Gaffga company was in business the Gaffga marine motors were noted as dependable, economical and efficient gasoline motors and were sold to customers in all parts of the country.

Several days ago, Mr. Gaffga received a post card from Fairfax, Minn. The writer of the card said that he had one of the company's 1916 catalogues and asked for a new catalogue. He also wrote that he had a four-horsepower Gaffga motor which he purchased second hand a number of years ago which was still in service in a 23-foot boat.

Sea Power and the Origin of the New York State Merchant Marine Academy

There was a time a century or more ago, when the strength and prosperity of a nation depended on a strong navy (think Theodore Roosevelt), which protected a large merchant marine fleet. (For example, without a strong navy, the Barbary Pirates ran wild praying upon our merchant vessels in the Mediterranean in the late 1700s.) See the *Six Frigates: The Epic History of the Founding of the U.S. Navy* by Ian W. Toll. Another classic book on the subject, *The Influence of Sea Power upon History* by Alfred T. Mahon documents how sea power has determined the course of world history for centuries. In response to this reality, a handful of states, including New York State, established state merchant marine academies.

My Dad as a cadet aboard the SS *Newport*.

My father at the Academy.

The school ship, the SS *Newport* sailed out of Bedloe's Island (since renamed Liberty Island) in New York Harbor where the Statue of Liberty stands. The *SS Newport* made an appearance in Greenport Harbor every summer before it departed on its annual cruise across the Atlantic to Europe. It was a beautiful three-masted sailing vessel that must have looked like a flying cloud when under full sail. For a young man, one of the greatest advertisements for a seagoing life was to witness the majestic presence of this three-masted ship at anchor in the harbor. A large part of the excitement was the races that were arranged between the ship's rowing team and any boat from town that wanted to take them on. The cadets looked tan and muscular compared to the young men in town and usually won the races.

The school ship—the SS *Newport*.

The presence of the *SS Newport* in plain view was like a siren call (think Lorelei on the Rhine River) to a young man beckoning him to visit far off, exotic lands. My father had seen the SS *Newport* in Greenport Harbor many times. He applied and was accepted to the New York State Merchant Marine Academy in the class of 1924. He made two voyages to Europe on the school ship, which is described in the book *Bob Graham at Sea* by Felix Riesenberg. "The best thing I ever did was to go to the Academy," my father said more than once.

Embedded in all of these nautical influences is what I believe is my reason for choosing to go to sea, whether it was my father's stories, the examples of what his extended family did in real life, or the opportunity to be part of their environment. I too wanted to sail the seven seas and see the world.

It's funny, I didn't realize the connection between my Navy experience and my roots on Long Island until I started to write this book. I had always taken my experiences for granted. When I finally asked myself where this desire to go to sea came from, I realized that it came to me through my father and his seafaring past.

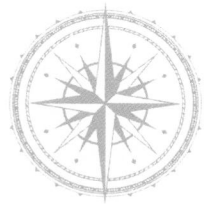

CHAPTER 2
From OCS to Guam—A Boot Ensign

I enlisted in the Navy right out of college. One of my best friends at Yale University, George Olson, and I went down to the recruiting office and enlisted together. This was in the spring of 1964 and there was a lot of talk about the conflict that was heating up in Vietnam. He got orders to flight school in Pensacola, Florida, and I got orders to Officer Candidate School (OCS) in Newport, Rhode Island. I had a report date in late October 1964, so I made the most of that summer, having fun while working as a Pinkerton guard at the New York World's Fair (GM Pavilion). On October 24, I took the train from my home on Long Island, New York to Providence, Rhode Island, via Penn Station in New York City.

Bob Henning and me, Officer Candidates home on Christmas

The ride from Providence to Newport (Rhode Island) took a bit longer than I anticipated. It was about 1800 (6:00 pm) when I arrived on base, just a few hours past my required reporting time. The thought occurred to me that I had already committed my first military infraction. But in the confusion with so many candidates arriving on the same day, my tardiness was not even noticed. As they arrived, the candidates were assigned to companies using letters of the alphabet; the early birds joined Alpha Company and I was assigned to Papa. The guys in Papa Company were in Papa Company for the same reason that I was—they had all reported around 1600 hours, late, but unnoticed. And maybe because of that characteristic, we found a way to get by without attracting too much attention, which is a good quality to have in the service because the program that lay ahead of us was 18 weeks of pure hell. You didn't want to be conspicuous.

That bit of wisdom notwithstanding, I accepted a nomination and was elected Yeoman for Papa Company. I had daily responsibilities but not more than I could handle.

Not everyone made it to graduation. We had a section leader with prior enlisted experience, Roger Eastman, who helped us get squared away. But apparently the additional burden of helping us proved to be too much for him and, unfortunately, he washed out of the program and was sent out to the fleet as a "white hat," an enlisted man who would probably be peeling potatoes on his first assignment at his first duty station. Anyway, that's what we believed would happen. Despite the loss of Roger as our leader, morale remained high. Our favorite song was *King of the Road* by Roger Miller which we sang in the barracks.

Our barracks was an old WWII wooden building with a large open bay with bunk beds. At night, the sound of 30 officer candidates sleeping sounded like a jungle orchestra. I slept soundly every night.

Upon graduation from OCS in March 1965, each of us in Papa Company received orders to various places around the globe—mostly ships homeported on the East Coast or the West Coast of the United States. Many of my classmates were assigned to attend Navy schools before reporting to their first duty station.

Naval Justice School in Newport.

I was ordered to report to Naval Justice School located on the base at Newport, and from there, to go on to Guam. Did they think I was smart or something? Thinking back to 1965, those were the days before an accused person had the legal right to be represented by a lawyer at a court-martial. It was also before the days when every accused person had to be read his rights before being questioned (Mirandized—"You have the right to remain silent, anything you say may be used against you in a court of law"). The *Miranda* decision by the Supreme Court would change all of that. Absent this right, my class at Justice School was made up of about half lawyers and half non-lawyers, all expected to perform similar legal duties upon graduation.

My "Used Car" Business

Sometime in late February 1965, just before graduating from Officer Candidate School, I bought my first car. It was a 1960 Chevrolet Biscayne with a three-speed manual shift on the column. It was reliable but not much to look at. For a lot of young Ensigns, their first car had to be a big status symbol such as an Oldsmobile 442 or a Datsun 280Z sports car. Having been just set free from 18 weeks in the confines of OCS and wanting to experience the freedom of cruising the nearby Newport area on weekends and after classes, my car was more for transportation. The only real trip I made was all the way to Poughkeepsie, New York to attend the prom with my not too serious girlfriend, Stephanie (from Shaker Heights, Michigan) who was a senior at Vassar. We enjoyed the weekend together and when she graduated, she took a job in Encino, California.

Our family car, a 1964 Oldsmobile convertible.

Before leaving for Guam, I returned home for a brief period to say goodbye to my family. My sister, Judy, was home for the summer from college at Davis and Elkins College in Elkins, West Virginia, and she needed transportation. So, when I left for Guam, she drove my Chevy and then took it back to West Virginia where she agreed to sell it and send me the proceeds. My used car was worth more there than on Long Island and she kept the sweetener, the amount above the price I paid for it in Rhode Island. As a bonus, she had free transportation for the summer and a way back to school in the fall. And later, I received my investment back from her—what a sister! I was just beginning to dip my little toe into the used car business.

I was headed to Guam. So, after a few days of leave at home on Long Island, I lined up transportation in New York City in a late model Plymouth Fury that the owner wanted delivered to his place of business on Wilshire Boulevard in Los Angeles (LA), California. I picked up the car in the city and drove cross-country from New York to LA; all I had to pay for, I thought, was gas. On the way, I traveled the famous Route 66 where the posted speed limit in the 1960s in Oklahoma was anything "reasonable and prudent." My progress became a bit dicey, however, as I approached Amarillo, Texas. The engine started to miss and then catch again, miss and then catch again. I quickly found a garage where they replaced the fuel pump, more or less, right away so I could be on my way again. With the defective fuel pump in the trunk and a receipt for the work in my pocket, I resumed my trip.

I found the address on Wilshire Boulevard and grabbed the defective fuel pump from the trunk. When I dropped the keys and the pump on the secretary's desk, she was more than happy to write me a check for the full replacement cost, which was a relief. Now, I was left standing on a street corner in LA with my luggage trying to figure out how I was going to get from LA to San Francisco to catch a flight to Guam. The obvious answer was—to buy a car, drive to San Francisco, and then ship the car to Guam. I laughed because that is what I had been trying to do - I just couldn't keep them very long and the one I was about to buy I got rid of pretty much immediately. I knew I was authorized to ship a car to Guam; my orders read "POV recommended." (POV in military talk means *Privately Owned Vehicle*.)

Deceived by the California Sun— Automobiles and Motorcycles

If you have been to LA, you probably know that it is very different compared to "back East." Among other things, these differences can be very deceiving. What I saw was hundreds and hundreds of used cars, all apparently in mint condition. LA must be the place with the largest selection of used cars a person could desire, all in great condition. I could now get the car I really wanted. Do you remember what a cool car the 1955 Chevy convertible looked like? I had my eye on a black one—the paint job was pristine. I took it for a test drive, bought it, and then headed north toward San Francisco. What a cool dude I was driving a convertible that I really liked with the top down. This one was coming to Guam with me!

My 1955 Chevy convertible.

I hadn't been on the road long, driving north on California Highway 101, when I began to realize that there was a mechanical problem with the transmission. My mood shifted from "cool dude" to "am I going to make it there?" I finally pulled into the YMCA in Oakland (California) and got a room, talked to some dudes, and pieced together what had happened: *I had been deceived by the California sun.* Compared to the Northeast where there's lots of rain, snow, and salt on the roads, within a few years, cars were eaten up with rust that we called body cancer. In Los Angeles, it is sunny (almost) every day, which is why the cars look brand new. Now I got it, the cars in LA were no better mechanically than a 10-year-old car in New York. What a blockhead I was!

The next step was to dispose of this car, and report to the base to get booked on a flight. I came across an Army guy from Fort Ord who was interested in buying the Chevy. After explaining the transmission problem, we struck a deal. He got the car and I took a hit on my investment. I agreed to mail him the paperwork which I did as soon as I got my title from the used car salesman in LA. I checked into Travis AFB and caught a flight the next day to Hickam Air Force Base in Hawaii.

A Stop in Hawaii

In Honolulu, I stayed with a high school friend who was stationed there. He was on the Admiral's staff, a position I believe he earned by being a standout tennis player in both high school and college. He and I met two girls from Canada at the YWCA—people from Canada love to vacation in Hawaii—and we hiked up to Sacred Falls on a river in the northern part of Oahu. I spent about 10 days with my friend, Forrest, in Honolulu at his place in the Queen Emma Apartments. During this time I took a side trip for a few days over to the big island on a Royal Hawaiian Airways flight. I stayed at a military facility called Kilauea Military Camp (KMC), where I rented a bike and rode the circumference of the Kilauea Volcano. The month before, in 1965, the volcano had exploded over 15 million cubic meters of lava. The eruption was preceded by an "inflation" of the Kilauea summit and then the collapse of the summit. This meant that the approaches to the caldera were fairly level, which allowed me to get close enough to see the molten lava inside. I took some pretty good pictures that I wish I could find now.

Kilauea Military Camp in Hawaii.

Footnote: Years later, when Cathy and I returned to the big island, we took a bus tour in the same area, where I saw a sign for Kilauea Military Camp. I asked the driver to stop and we got out and walked around a bit—I was pretty excited to see such a place decades later.

The used car business continued as I searched for a POV to ship to Guam. What I found was a Corvair Lakewood station wagon—the car with the engine in the rear. Ralph Nader saw fit to write about it in his famous book entitled *Unsafe at Any Speed*. The paint was rusting through and it wasn't very elegant;

this car obviously did not spend much time grooming itself in LA. I drove it down to the naval facility and convinced one of the bureaucrats there to ship it to Guam for me.

I Arrived on Guam in the Middle of the Night

In the morning, I woke up hot and sticky in the Bachelor Officer Quarters at the U.S. Naval Communications Station on the island of Guam . . .Guam, threatened by North Korean missiles in early 2019 and located in the Western Pacific is just a few degrees north of the equator. There was no air conditioning. I recall feeling the same uncomfortable heat that I had felt the night before when I arrived and descended the stairs of the military charter aircraft (World Airways) in almost total darkness. That morning, as I picked my shirt up off the chair to get dressed, there on the seat cushion was a lizard-like thing the likes of which I had never seen before. What the heck was it? Poisonous? I hadn't a clue. It struck me then that this city boy from New York had a lot to learn during the next 18 months, or however long Uncle Sam chose to keep me on this remote island.

A lizard-like thing I had never seen before, poisonous?

Reporting for Duty and "Old Salts"

But for now, I had to get dressed and report for duty as Personnel and Legal Officer at this tiny Communications Station halfway around the world. For a split second, I thought this could be a pretty good adventure. That thought vaporized almost immediately, because truthfully, at that moment I was more concerned with what the Navy expected from me, a brand-spanking new Ensign who was a lowly "Reservist" to boot. I could just imagine how some of the "old salts," who had made the Navy a career, would have fun with the likes of me. I reminded myself about what we had been taught at OCS: "Act like you know what you are doing. Somebody will correct you soon enough and you can learn from that." At the moment, that advice seemed like precious little to hold onto.

My Corvair Lakewood station wagon.

Car meets cow

When the Corvair finally arrived on Guam, I primed the rust spots and she was "good to go"—although she looked like she had the chicken pox. One night, four of us were returning to the Communication Station after dark from an event down the road. Guam is an "open range" territory, which means that cattle do not have to be fenced in on grazing land, so the cattle can wander freely over the island. It was raining hard and it was difficult to see—suddenly, I sideswiped a cow on the left side of the Corvair. Aside from some scratches on the door, I lost my rearview mirror. Everyone was safe and we continued back to the station. The cow appeared to be OK.

One of the biggest sporting activities on the island was football with each command fielding a team. The Air Force base had a team (or two, I don't remember,) the Naval Air Station had one, as did the Naval Station, the Communication Station, and so on. Since the football season corresponded with the rainy season, most of the games were played in the rain—messy!

Honda CB72 Superhawk scrambler.

On the civilian side, the most popular sport was drag racing on several of the many airstrips left over from WWII. For the junior officers, four or five of us would rent small scrambler motorcycles and have fun tooling around the hills out in the boonies. We scaled some pretty steep hills. Eventually, I bought a used Honda CB72 Superhawk scrambler from Special Services, probably owned by a sailor who did not want to bother shipping it back to the states. It didn't run that well, a problem I cured by cleaning out the gas tank with solvents and Drano. Notice in the photograph above how far away the person standing at the bottom of the hill appears to be—they were really steep hills.

A Mazda with a Wankel Engine

The next vehicle I purchased was from William (Bill) English Walling, a junior officer who was rotating back to the states. The guy had a colorful personality. He was the Communications Duty Officer and would often ask for a volunteer in his watch section to get him a cheeseburger from the Duva Den, the snack bar on the Communications Station. When no one volunteered, he would say, "OK, I've shown you my velvet glove, now I have no choice but to show you my iron fist." For all his bluster, he most likely got someone to get him his cheese-burger. For a POV, Bill had a most unusual car, a Mazda with a bubble dome and a Wankel engine in the rear. But he waited too long to find a serious buyer before his rotation date back to the states, so I got the car for a good price. I will talk more about vehicles in later chapters.

Investigating a Death on Guam

On my first day on the job, I was thrust into a case investigating a death. Four sailors left a popular Guamanian watering hole, "Pirates Cove," and climbed into a pickup truck—all were apparently drunk—two in the front seat and the other two in the bed of the truck. The truck peeled out of the gravel parking lot, skidded, then flipped over, and one of the passengers in the back hit his head and died. I was assigned to investigate the incident with Lt. Charlie Moon, a communications officer on the station. We submitted a report charging the driver with drunk driving and manslaughter. The accused sailor was shipped off for prosecution to another, larger base on the island and found guilty.

The bulk of my work as a legal officer was preparing and presenting cases at Captain's Mast, a form of nonjudicial punishment peculiar to the Navy. Typical punishments included a reduction in pay grade and/or a monetary fine. Confinement to the brig was authorized but almost never imposed. It was a delight to work with Captain Provost, the Commanding Officer, who was tough but fair with the men who appeared before him at Captain's Mast.

In one particular case, a sailor went missing (unauthorized absence) for about 2 months. During the interim, there was no word of what happened to him. This was not a Bowe Bergdahl stunt, and no one was killed looking for him, but it was still pretty serious, nevertheless. He had a girlfriend somewhere on the island, which is where they probably hid out together. As I recall, he came back to the base for some dental work and wound up at Captain's Mast.

Occasionally, a sailor would come to my office "in love" with the intention of marrying a local girl and taking her home to the states. In accordance with station policy, it was my duty to discourage this. But truth be told, sometimes the couples succeeded. I personally know such a couple, who were married on Guam and now live around the corner from us in Sun City, South Carolina. Jack was a junior officer when I was there, and Pauline was a Guamanian from the Calvo family. They celebrated 51 years of marriage before Pauline died earlier in 2018.

Although I was a Personnel and Legal Officer, I had no training in the personnel side of the job. I would just have to learn that from the enlisted men in my department as there were no other personnel or legal types at the Communications Station.

On the legal side of the department, I conducted the investigative work while my First-Class Yeoman (YN1) Johnston handled the paperwork. Of course, I reviewed everything. For official proceedings, he used a stenomask to record testimony before transcribing it to print. As mentioned, one very popular pursuit on Guam was drag racing. Johnston competed in his Mercury Comet.

First Class Yeoman (YN1) Johnston, legal Yeoman.

Another "sport" that I had never seen was cockfighting. I recall lots of money changing hands among the onlookers before the fight, and the owner of a bird stitching up his rooster after the bird lost a fight. I don't know if cock-fighting was legal or not when I was there—probably not.

For the personnel part of the job, I often relied on Personnelman First Class (PN1) Peters who knew the BuPers Manual (Bureau of Personnel) cold, especially how to interpret some of its arcane language. Among the many things I learned from him: When the manual says, "It may be required," it usually means *it is required*. I was fortunate to have good people working in my department, including three other PN types. The whole department worked "tropical hours," which meant we started an hour earlier in the morning and finished an hour earlier in the afternoon. We were trying to avoid the worst of the tropical heat—year-round. Not only was there no air conditioning in the Bachelor Officer Quarters (BOQ), there was also no air conditioning in the administration building.

Boonie stomping group.

Boonie Stomping in the Jungle

For recreation, a few of us junior officers would organize a "boonie stomp" somewhere on the island, which was about 28 miles in length and 7 miles wide. We explored rivers, caves, jungles, waterfalls, and beautiful sandy beaches. We also went horseback riding. Jack Zefutie had found some horses that we rented from a woman who lived on the island in a cave!

In the 1960s, many Guamanians lived a very primitive lifestyle. Guamanians have the same legal status as the citizens of Puerto Rico, as both Guam and Puerto Rico are overseas territories of the United States. Their culture is proud and strong. Family ties are paramount. To know a Guamanian female, you should be properly introduced to her.

Jack Zefutie and me tubing on a river.

In retrospect, Guam was a tropical paradise. Geographically, there was a high, grassy plateau in the north and rugged jungle-covered terrain in the south. The environment was relatively unspoiled, with tropical vegetation throughout. A road ran around the circumference of the island with beautiful views at every turn. And contrary to reports from recent visitors to Guam, there were no snakes at all on the island when I was there. They were introduced much later and had a devastating effect on the local bird population. Wild boar roamed free.

Diving from a waterfall (red circle).

Tuba Beer and Betel Nuts

Coconut trees abounded and the islanders used the coconuts to make tuba beer. Betel nuts were also found on the island, which the natives (and some of our sailors) chewed for a mild high. As legal officer, I had to decide whether betel nuts should be classed as a narcotic and therefore be prohibited for use by U.S. sailors aboard the station. In making this decision I was relying on the fact that the U.S. drug culture of the 1960s had not yet impacted life on Guam. I classified it as a narcotic.

The population on the island was about evenly split between Micronesian islanders and U.S. military personnel with a sprinkling of civilians, many of whom were tech reps for the military. For some reason, we referred to these civilians as "sand crabs." It is interesting to note that there were no tourists on the island and therefore no hotels. The only regular civilian airline service to the island was a Pan American flight that landed once a week, which stayed overnight to rest the crew and refuel the plane.

The lack of tourists meant that we had miles and miles of beautiful, deserted sandy beaches protected by a coral reef all to ourselves. Snorkeling in these tropical waters, we saw schools of tropical fish, sea anemone, and shells on the floor of quiet lagoons protected from the surf by an extensive reef in many places.

Ritidian Point, Guam, we go diving in a cave,
the water pool has not bottom, 1966

SCUBA diving in Ritidian Cave.

A Freshwater Pool inside a Cave

Caves were hard to find and could be dangerous. Some were inhabited by hundreds of bats that hung from the ceiling and other caves were so inaccessible that there was no life whatsoever inside. We found one cave with a freshwater pool inside. We brought in SCUBA gear. The water was crystal clear but black as coal for lack of light. I took the picture above of the first two guys when they descended. When it was my turn to go down, I was initially disoriented by the total blackness. My buddies held flashlights at the top so, when I looked up, I could get my bearings. What we discovered was that there was no bottom to the pool. It was too risky to go down any further, so we surfaced and called it a day.

A Brush with My Own Death

My closest brush with death occurred in a cave on Thanksgiving Day in 1965. I was sharing some of our exploits in caves with a new Ensign, Jay Colden, who had just reported aboard the station. He was interested in seeing the caves, so I agreed to take him to Ritidian Cave in the jungle on the northwest corner of the island. I had been there before. But very foolishly, I said this time we could make the trip with only candles for light. After exploring the floor of the cave which was strewn with huge boulders underneath the large cathedral ceiling, we headed back in the direction of the entrance. It was not there! Suddenly, we faced a stone wall where the entrance should have been. For the next several hours we alternately put out our candles, searched for a point of light, then tried to relight the candles with matches that were by now damp with perspiration. Then we waited for what seemed like hours for the matches to dry a bit. Finally we were able to relight our candles, and miraculously we were able to walk straight to the opening. It took a lot of concentration to fight back the urge to panic; I instinctively wanted to reach for a phone, but I kept my cool and evaluated our best chances for getting out. With much relief, we return to the base to enjoy Thanksgiving dinner.

Footnote: In my caving experiences on Guam, I encountered two dimensions of danger as described above: Diving in a bottomless pool of water with SCUBA gear and becoming disoriented; and on another occasion, being unable to find the exit in a pitch-black cave for several hours. Thus ended for all intents and purposes my desire to go spelunking.

Thailand (July 2018)

You have probably heard the story of a boys youth soccer team that was trapped 2.5 miles underground in a cave for 2 weeks. Their unflooded sheltering space was reduced to 108 square feet by rising waters. In one story, I read that some of the boys reported hearing chickens and cows. After hiking in with their coach, monsoon rains flooded the cave and an international rescue effort was mounted to save them. They all escaped but they endured the hardships that the ordeal implies: lack of food, water, light, and even dangerously low levels of oxygen. For example, they drank water that dripped off the stalactites hanging from the ceiling.

This story which took place in Thailand confirmed just how dangerous my own caving experiences were in Guam. But I still wondered—how did they keep it together for 2 weeks? Did they have the irresistible urge to reach for a phone as I did? Or, did they just hear chickens and cows? You can learn a lot from adversity. Culture informs our imagination under stress. I am grateful to be alive.

An Ill-Fated Cruise to Cocos Island

Guam, enroute to Cocos Island, 1966

Opening day on Cocos Island Recreation Area.

The civil engineers on Guam had just opened up a recreation facility on Cocos Island off the southern tip of the island located within the Merizo Barrier Reef. It was open to the public, so on opening day there was an assorted group of people that wanted to go, civilians and military alike. We boarded an old WWII landing craft. It must have been an important event because we had a helicopter escort that monitored our progress.

Guam, helo escort on the way to Cocos Island, 1966

A helicopter monitors our progress.

Several of us junior officers from the Communications Station (Jack Zefutie, Jim Sharples, and I) were aboard. We brought along a rubber raft along because we expected to be in the water most of the day. Coral grows in abundance in the shallow waters around Guam, and Cocos Island was no exception.

We were in shallow water that was about 4 feet deep as the landing craft approached the shoreline of Cocos Island. Even at a slow speed, there was a big "thump" as the landing craft came to a complete and sudden stop. It was hung up on a coral head and couldn't move, forward and couldn't move backward. The only movement it could make was to spin around when the engines accelerated. The boat was stuck fast for the duration. What a sight that was.

Finally, I tossed our raft overboard and the three of us took turns scoping out the situation. The landing craft was still stuck, so eventually we paddled ashore and made a day of it on the beach.

Guam, landing craft gets stuck on a coral head, and I take off in my rubber raft. 1966

I tossed our raft overboard for a better view of the situation.

Side Note: The landing craft was known as a Landing Craft, Vehicle, Personnel (LCVP) or a Higgins Boat named after its inventor, Andrew Higgins. Developed in the 1930s for use in the Gulf of Mexico, it was used in all the amphibious landings in WWII and is credited as "the boat that won the war." It draws about 3 feet of water and should have been perfect to land us on Cocos Island, except for the coral head that we struck. The LCVP is featured in a WWII museum in New Orleans including an authentic example complete with all its particulars.

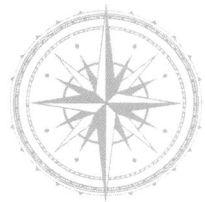

CHAPTER 3

Liberation Day on Guam and Dissent Back Home

WWII and the Japanese Occupation

At the very start of World War II (December 1941), Japan invaded and occupied Guam. Torture and death became a daily incident in almost every large community, and the degradation of a gentle, peaceful people became a chronic affair. Perhaps the blackest days of Guam's long and chaotic history during the war were those endless months between spring and summer of 1944 when the population suffered the extreme miseries of occupation while awaiting the return of their American protectors.

Father Duenas headed up the Guamanian resistance.

From the beginning, in December 1941, Father Jesus Baza Duenas headed up the resistance. He confronted Japanese officials at every turn. Fr. Duenas did what he could to stand up to injustice whenever he encountered it. He quickly became a thorn in the side of the Japanese. But it was his alleged knowledge of the whereabouts of George Tweed, an American sailor hiding out in the jungle that was his biggest liability. Tweed had escaped capture by the Japanese, aided by friendly Chamorro people who assisted him with food and shelter. They confided in him and he had them to thank for saving his life. George Tweed was rescued when the Americans retook the island, but by then Fr. Duenas had been captured and beheaded by the Japanese. There is a shrine to his memory in the village of Inarajan located on the south end of the island. I hope to visit there when I go back to Guam.

Liberation

In a campaign of bloody warfare that began on July 21, 1944 and lasted 3 weeks, American forces assaulted the beaches and regained control of the island. They landed tanks and personnel carriers ashore and pushed inland. There were fierce tank battles that raged on the northern part of the island, where the land was flat and covered with elephant grass. We saw blown-up tanks with holes in the turrets that had pierced several inches of armor. There were 1,800 U.S. servicemen killed and 7,400 total U.S. casualties. Guam was liberated and peace returned to the island. (The guy in the photo in red, our friend Forest Rieber, looks like he just liberated a donut shop, not an island; I appear on the right.)

We found shot-up tanks and personnel carriers.

A Japanese Straggler 28 Years Later

In 1972, long after my tour of duty there had ended, American newspapers told of a Japanese soldier that was still holding out on Guam. Shoichi Yokoi was a tailor from Tokyo who had served in the 38th Infantry Regiment of the old Imperial Japanese Army. He lived in the jungle around Talofofo Bay on a diet of mangos, nuts, crabs, prawns, snails, rats, eels, pigeons, and wild hog. We had explored his river, his bay, and his waterfall many times. He must have seen us, but of course, he never revealed himself. Did he know that WWII was over? Of course. Was he willing to surrender? No, that would be dishonorable. After what the Japanese occupiers had done to the Guamanian population, perhaps he feared for his life.

Shoichi Yokoi from the Japanese Army.

As a footnote to this story, the Japanese acclaimed their unique *"Yamato spirit,"* and willed themselves to believe that it must deliver ultimate victory. *At home and on the front lines* the Japanese would endure privations and hardships that the enemy could never withstand—they would work harder, eat less, and face death with samurai-like indifference. They would strive harder to find the motivation to overcome whatever difficulties they encountered. They abhorred retreat or surrender. This was what Shoichi Yokoi was living up to when he hid out in the jungle for 28 years. But peace and freedom had already won out over hate and butchery long before his surrender.

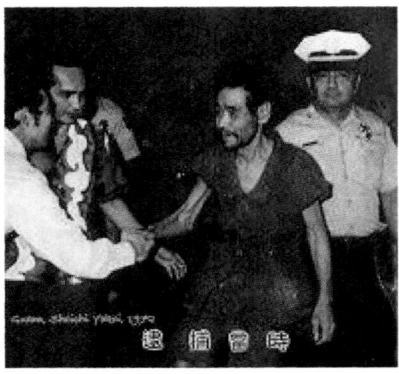

Shoichi Yokoi surrenders, 1972.

The Liberation Day Celebration

The impact of the war years in Guam has been turned into an enduring celebration of goodwill. The major celebration on Guam is Liberation Day. It makes me happy to know that this event, after all these years, continues to be a major celebration on the island.

I wondered what the celebration was like this year (in 2018). I read online that this year, the residents and visitors crowded the streets and sidewalks of Marine Corps Drive from Adelup to the Chamorro Village for the parade. It is still the day the Chamorro people rejoice and celebrate the liberation of Guam from Japanese rule 74 years ago. There were 53 group participants in the parade, said Dededo Mayor Melissa Savares. There were 15 civilian float entries—six village floats, four floats from nonprofit groups, and five from GovGuam agencies.

Enthusiasm for the celebration has not waned.

My date—Addie Certeza.

Back in 1966, some of the junior officers were tapped to be escorts for the contestants in the Miss Liberation Day contest. My contestant was a pretty island girl from the village of Asan. She still lives on Guam today, in the village of Dededo. The men wore their dress white uniforms with swords and behaved as perfect gentlemen. As I recall, the winner was a girl named Scholastica.

Miss Liberation Day, Scholastica.

Although there was very little mixing between the local population and the military when I was there, one tradition stood out. Once a month (during the year), one of the dozen or so villages on the island would open their homes to visitors and serve delicious Guamanian delicacies. The junior officers from the Naval Communications Station always felt welcome at these festivals.

Miss Liberation Day ceremonies.

Isolated from the Outside World

In a time before the general use of satellites, we were isolated: no television, no radio from the outside world. The only news from the outside world was from magazines that arrived on the island about a month late. The photographs we took around the island had to be sent to San Francisco for processing, so they were late as well. Kodak slides were all the rage and we would get together, sometimes at the home of one of the junior officers who was married and eligible for base housing and play "keno" or watch slides of our exploits on a Kodak carousel. For young married couples, a tour on Guam could be a prolonged honeymoon on a tropical island away from family. Calling home to talk to mom was prohibitive at $12 a minute, so the young couples had to work out their problems on their own. I think nowadays, working out your own problems would be called "growing up."

After the ceremonies, the junior officers gathered for beers.

Demonstrations and Dissent Back Home

One of these couples, arriving on Guam for their first tour of duty, told of dissent and demonstrations against the war in Vietnam that had begun to occur on the campus at Berkeley (1966). (The Vietnam War had only escalated to become a war at about the time I arrived on Guam.) Dissent and demonstrations (that I know of) had not occurred before I left the states in April of 1965. The momentous cultural changes of the 1960s had begun and were passing me by while I was out of the country. And more importantly, we didn't understand the demonstrations, maybe because we didn't see the horror of battle as it was presented on the 6:00 o'clock news every night in the living rooms of people back home.

I should also mention that the "Cultural Revolution" also began at about the same time in China. It made very little sense to us on Guam because it was instigated and directed by Mao Zedong, who was in-charge of China. The bloated bureaucracy was stagnant. In an effort to make China more responsive to his leadership, he sought to neutralize those groups that opposed him. Universities were closed and professors were sent to rural communes for indoctrination. Learning stopped. Offices were closed. This happened because the bureaucracy failed to move the country away from ancient traditional ways. Production of just about everything fell into serious decline. Starvation and disease followed. Millions died. I also missed the great blackout that occurred up and down the East Coast of the United States in late 1965. Isolated we were.

A giant waterspout seen from our Beechcraft on the way to Saipan.

Reaching Out across the South Pacific

Before leaving Guam, I was interested in visiting other South Pacific Islands. I found a local pilot with a Beechcraft King Air that seated eight, he was making a run to the island of Saipan although I don't recall whether it was part of a scheduled airline flight or not. On the way to Saipan, we flew over the island of Rota, which is about 40 miles north of Guam. From the shore of the northern end of Guam Rota looks like two separate islands, two hills separated by water. But from the air Rota is clearly one island. So much for the "flat Earth" theory.

About halfway into the 1-hour flight, I witnessed one of those wonders of nature—a giant waterspout touched the waters of the Pacific as it soared to great heights in the sky. As we approached Saipan, I could see the island of Tinian off to the left. I was looking at a part of history—the place where Paul Tibbets took off in the Enola Gay with the first atomic bomb, which was used to destroy Hiroshima. Saipan had been a Japanese possession since the end of WWI, and I could see the high cliff where the Japanese rulers of the island jumped to their deaths rather than surrender to the invading American forces. When I return to Guam with Cathy someday, I would like to take her on an excursion to Saipan and go back to a place in time where Western development has yet to reach.

During my tour of duty on Guam, I had two opportunities to go on leave for "Rest & Recreation"—Japan and Hong Kong. I flew to a U.S. base, Yakota, in Japan with my friend Bob Schrage, and we stayed in Tokyo. At that time, the U.S. dollar was trading at 360 yen. The dollar was king, and Japan and Hong Kong were fabulous places to shop for anything.

A Unique Japanese Experience

A Japanese garden in Kyoto.

The highlight of the trip was my visit to Kyoto on the high-speed bullet train with one stop at Nagoya. The rock gardens and coy ponds in Kyoto were so artistically done, a beautiful and uniquely Japanese experience for someone who had never traveled outside of the United States before. In fact, I fell in love with Japan and even had the chance to return before too long (Chapter 4).

I found a large park and observed what looked like groups of pilgrims following a holy man—or maybe he was just a tour guide—along narrow paths. The only way to describe what I saw is to share the amazing photographs.

Japanese pilgrims in Kyoto.

Hong Kong Bargains

Months later, on May 27, 1966, I traveled to Hong Kong where I stayed at the August Moon Hotel and rode the White Star Ferry between the island of Hong Kong and an area on the mainland called Kowloon. Hong Kong was well known for its custom-tailored clothing and shoes. Besides two pair of boots and a custom-made suit, I went to Vashe Tailors where I had half-a-dozen shirts tailored from fine Oxford broadcloth. What a treat. Those shirts lasted well into my first job at IBM, which I didn't start until 1970. I also bought china and silk for my family. In the midst of great wealth of this British crown colony, there was also poverty. This photo was taken in front of my hotel, the August Moon. The vehicle in the picture is the hotel shuttle.

A homeless mother and baby outside my hotel, the Teahouse of the August Moon, in Hong Kong.

I Strike a Deal for My Next Duty Station

After a year and a half on Guam, I received orders for my next duty station. The orders were not what I had hoped for—I wanted to see as much of the world as I could, which meant sea duty. I called my detailer in Washington to negotiate a better deal. I had to place the call from Guam to Washington, DC in the middle of the night as Guam is on the other side of the world—south of Japan and east of the Philippine Islands. I told him that I wanted to be on a ship that would be covering a lot of geography. He offered me the USS *Franklin D. Roosevelt* (CVA-42), an aircraft carrier based on the East Coast, in exchange for 6 months of additional service. I am the only person I know who extended his obligated service time in exchange for duty in a war zone off the coast of Vietnam. My reasoning was simple—I didn't think the Navy would chance losing a carrier even if it were in a combat zone. So, I reckoned it was a good deal, accepted the orders, and my adventure continued.

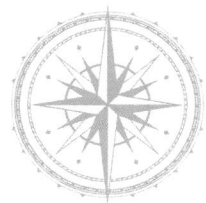

CHAPTER 4

The Tonkin Gulf—A Young Man Goes to Sea

S ometime during my first tour of duty in the U.S. Navy on Guam in the far Pacific, I made two important decisions: The first was to go to sea and the second was to finish what I had already started, namely, a circumnavigation of the world by traveling west. With my orders in hand, I made my way from Guam to the Philippine Islands where I boarded a Navy ship, the USS *Intrepid*, bound for the Tonkin Gulf. (I have omitted the part of the story of how I got from Guam to the Philippines; that is another complete chapter in itself.)

Reporting Aboard the Roosevelt

After 4 days on the USS *Intrepid* (CVS-11), I retrieved my seabag and climbed up to the flight deck in preparation for the short helo ride to the USS *Franklin D. Roosevelt* (*FDR*) (CVA-42), which would be my home for the next 2 years. The seas were calm. The rotor blades of the helo were turning as I climbed aboard. We lifted off the deck of the Intrepid just a stone's throw from the Roosevelt. I could see the Roosevelt, but I knew something wasn't right with the *FDR—she wasn't moving*! Now that I had finally arrived on Yankee Station in the Tonkin Gulf aboard the Intrepid, there was the *Roosevelt*—"waiting"—in fact she was "dead in the water."

While checking in aboard ship I was directed to the Photo Lab. Divers had just returned with photographs of the number 1 propeller; one of its blades had broken off. We headed for Yokosuka, Japan where there was a dry dock that was large enough to accommodate our aircraft carrier and a replacement propeller could be found. The dry dock was actually built to accommodate 85,000-ton battleships built by the Japanese before and during WWII. (The *Roosevelt* was a mere 62,000 tons fully loaded.)

Yokosuka, Japan, number 1 propeller replaced.

Caught in a Typhoon

As we steamed north toward Japan, we ran into a typhoon—Typhoon Nancy. (It would be the first of two I encountered on the ship, the other being Pamela.) A typhoon in the Pacific is the same type of weather system as a hurricane in the Atlantic. Two destroyers were in company with the *FDR*, but try as we might, there was no course we could steer that would provide a comfortable ride for the destroyers. Those "tin-can" sailors were pretty wet, cold, and seasick by the time we reached Japan. The aircraft carrier was significantly larger and a lot more stable, so we didn't take near the soaking that those sailors did. These were the days before operational satellites, which probably would have reported the serious weather conditions to the navigator and thus allowed us to take evasive action.

Encounter with Typhoon Nancy on the way to Japan.

Had I arrived onboard the *FDR* one day later, I would have missed the entire diversion to Japan. As it was, we wound up safely in dry dock in Yokosuka. Repairs took about a week and I used my liberty time to see the Great Buddha at Kamakura and the sailboats at Enoshima, both easily reachable from Yokosuka. This was my second visit to Japan, this one by ship.

Great Buddha at Kamakura, Japan.

Yokosuka

The honey wagon makes a pick-up.

After liberty call, I often walked around one of the residential neighborhoods in Yokosuka. It was worth the 20-minute wait to see the man exit the house across the street with two honey buckets balanced across his shoulders.

During my walks in the immediate area, it was evident that zoning standards in Yokosuka were either nonexistent or very loosely enforced. Although it was not one of the better neighborhoods, I still felt safe—it was almost like the residents understood that we (the United States) were now the protectors of their nation that was so recently devastated in WWII. This was true in a bygone (post–WWII) age of overwhelming American military power. I believe, and I think history confirms, that in Japan's case we used our power wisely.

Exploring a neighborhood in Yokosuka, Japan

Carrying the War to the Japanese Homeland

Built for the invasion of the Japanese home islands, the *Roosevelt* had many unique features including a steel flight deck that would have rendered a kamikaze attack less lethal. (Until then, the flight decks of U.S. carriers were made of wood such as the flight deck of the *Intrepid*.) Especially significant for protecting an aircraft carrier is its ability to detect and react to incoming threats at a distance from the aircraft carrier. This is accomplished by the Combat Information Center and Airborne Early Warning (AEW), both of which are defensive features in addition to the steel flight deck.

Nerve Center of the Ship—The Combat Information Center (CIC)

The *Roosevelt* was already on station off the coast of North Vietnam when I reported onboard. I was assigned to work in the Combat Information Center (CIC), which tracks all aircraft and ships within a 40/60-mile radius. Our mission in CIC was to detect and react to threats before they got too close. (Our modern-day Navy is still working to get this right—witness the number of U.S. Navy collisions at sea in recent years.)

The Combat Information Center (CIC) on the *Roosevelt*.

I worked with the surface picture where our main input, minute by minute, was a surface search radar repeater. In those days, we used grease pencils on the face of radar repeaters (the center of the image) and parallel rulers to connect several plots in order to calculate the *course and speed of each contact*. (If you look closely, you can see a grease pencil on the radar repeater.) This information was then posted for display on a tote board, again using a grease pencil. Each number was written backward. (Even a complex wind problem can be solved with a grease pencil and a set of parallel rulers.) Do electronic readouts of courses and speeds help the CIC Officer to keep the tactical (surface) picture in mind? I'd like to have a debate on that subject with a guy from today's navy. The CIC worked closely with the navigation bridge on every phase of "ship driving." (Piloting takes information from fixed markers on land while Ship Driving takes place in the blue water out at sea.) Pete Gutschneider who worked with me in the CIC (pictured on the right in the photo above) and I became friends and then roommates. He was a good guy to know, and we remain friends to this day. (Unfortunately, Pete died on Memorial Day, 2019.)

When the ship turned into the wind to launch aircraft, a Russian trawler, typically the *Bargraph*, would oftentimes try to disrupt our air operations by deliberately stationing itself directly in the Roosevelt's path, thereby risking a collision. You can imagine the tension on the navigation bridge and in CIC when this happened. There was absolute quiet except for range and bearing markers called out as the two ships drew closer. The Russians invariably backed off as we had the right-away while operating aircraft.

Airborne Early Warning Planes

Even without a direct enemy threat to our mission, things sometimes went wrong and sometimes went wrong with dire consequences. We had two Grumman Airborne Early Warning (AEW) planes onboard nicknamed "Willie Fudd" for the large radar dome that was mounted above the fuselage. Each plane carried a crew of four. Their mission was to scout, find, and report distant threats so we that could effectively coordinate a defensive response.

One of the Grumman Airborne Early Warning planes, Willie Fudd.

Once, one of the Willie Fudds was returning to the ship and its landing gear was jammed in the *up* position. A decision was made to ditch the plane in the water astern of the *Roosevelt*. In hindsight, such a decision was to exercise that oxymoronic trick known as a "water landing." The plane flipped over, sank and all four men aboard were lost. That day, I lost a friend—Dick Mowrey—who was in the crew.

In a letter to his parents, the Commanding Officer of the ship, Martin G. O'Neill, wrote in part: "... our mission in the Gulf of Tonkin and the sacrifices of men, like your son, gave the full measure of devotion to make that mission a success." Dick Mowrey was a friend I have never forgotten. Dick and I had gone on liberty together in the Philippines.

At night when we were not operating aircraft, we would steam at darken ship with lookouts posted at port and starboard. One dark night, the starboard lookout called out, "Sail ho, starboard bow." A few minutes later, the port side lookout reported a second contact to port. Then other sightings started checking in. We had steamed into a North Vietnamese fishing fleet whose boats and sails did not show up on our radar.

I was on watch on the bridge, so I walked over to the flying bridge on the starboard side and was immediately looking straight down into the faces of several North Vietnamese fishermen. The side of their boat was painted with the face and body of a ferocious, red Chinese dragon, probably to ward off evil spirits. As I took in the sight, I realized that this was going to be a peaceful encounter with mutual benefits to both parties and without hostility.

Bob Hope's Christmas Show aboard the *FDR* in the Tonkin Gulf.

Amidst the challenges of operating under wartime conditions, the crew enjoyed a welcome reprieve when Bob Hope and his Christmas Show boarded the ship to entertain us when we were still on Yankee Station off the coast of North Vietnam. Along with Bob Hope were Phyllis Diller, Anita Bryant with her powerful voice, Joey Heatherton—a dancer, Reita Faria—Miss World 1966 from India, and the Korean Kittens. It was a fine show. (I first saw Bob Hope's Christmas Show a year earlier when I was stationed on Guam.)

Beans, Bullets, and Black Oil

It has been said that the Navy runs on *beans*, *bullets*, and *black oil*. Still bound by that old maxim, the *Roosevelt* would "shop" at sea about once a week, pulling up alongside an underway replenishment ship to take on groceries, ammunition, or fuel. "Groceries" here refers to all supplies beyond ammunition and fuel. I have even seen personnel high lined across from ship to ship sitting in a bosun's chair.

We would rendezvous while steaming at 12 knots, sent over a messenger line, and then make fast heavier lines at both ends that allowed us to set up a pulley system to haul over the heavy skids loaded with our groceries. At other times, this same procedure was repeated with ammunition ships to load heavy ordnance (bombs and rockets) aboard. In addition, we would pull up alongside an oiler to refuel with black oil, jet fuel, and aviation gasoline.

Refueling Our Destroyers

Once we were refueled, our accompanying destroyers would pull up alongside the *Roosevelt* to receive fuel directly from the carrier on an "as needed" basis using the same procedure that was used with the oiler. Note the hose hanging from the span wire in three places—the seas were not always as rough as they are in the above photograph. Each evolution with an "unrep" ship would take about 4 hours to complete in addition to the daily 8 hours of flight operations. After an underway replenishment, it could easily take a day or two to break down the skids and properly stowed everything below the decks. Until that was accomplished you might see a young sailor eating his meal on the mess decks while sitting on a 500-pound bomb. The food on a carrier, by the way, was generally considered excellent.

Refueling while underway in rough weather.

Hong Kong and a Risky Bargain

The floating city of Aberdeen.

One of the highlights of this cruise for me was our visit to Hong Kong which, in the 1960s, was already a booming, modern city. This was my second visit, this on by sea. We dropped anchor in the harbor, lowered our small personnel boats into the water, and made our way to the pier for liberty. This being my second visit to what was then still a British crown colony, I could find my way around with no trouble. I visited both the island side of Hong Kong and the mainland side—Kowloon. We saw the floating city of Aberdeen, and the poverty of the people who spent their entire lives on boats, called "junks." Think of how public health is affected without adequate sewage disposal. For a very low fare, travel back and forth between the island and the mainland was easy on the White Star Ferry. I understand that in 2018, a tunnel connecting the island of Hong Kong and the mainland opened.

We take a strain and lift my motorcycle.

Beyond Kowloon were the New Territories, where I ventured in search of my second motorcycle. (My first motorcycle was the one I owned in Guam). I found a Honda motorcycle dealership in the Yellow Pages, took a cab and found the dealer who spoke Chinese; more properly—he *only* spoke Chinese. Still, we managed to work out a deal for the motorcycle I wanted. I paid 50 percent down, drew a picture of an aircraft carrier on a piece of paper and penciled in the number "42" on the island superstructure. I felt "OK" with the arrangements and caught a cab back to the pier.

The dealer was supposed to deliver my motorcycle to the ship on the morning we were supposed to weigh anchor and get underway. I paced the quarterdeck watching for him and checking my watch. There was no one in sight. Then, I spied a Chinese junk moving slowly toward the *Roosevelt*. Aboard was a family—father, mother, and their two Chinese daughters all wearing the typical Chinese coolie hats. And there on the deck sat a wooden crate with the motorcycle dealer standing next to it like a sentinel, whose only duty was to guard the container.

Figure 1 Motorcycle salesman in light coat waves goodbye.

I trusted the dealer and he delivered

I descended the ladder, shook hands with the dealer, smiled, and motioned to him to standby for the ship's crane. I had already cleared this with the deck division officer, so the crane operator was ready—and he lowered the hook, picked up the crate and raised it to the flight deck. I paid the dealer the other 50 percent, and my treasure was then stowed many decks below in an empty ammunition magazine. I am fairly sure this type of vehicle transport would not be allowed in today's Navy.

CHAPTER 5
Across the Equator and Around the World

Having completed our assigned tour of duty in the Tonkin Gulf, the *Roosevelt* set sail for the states on January 2, 1967. We began the long journey across the South China Sea and the Indian Ocean, then northwest up the length of the Atlantic Ocean—a journey that took us more than halfway around the world. Passing through the Sunda Strait between Java and Sumatra, we observed the site of Krakatoa, the volcano that erupted in 1883. The massive eruption killed more than 30,000 people, blanketing the Earth's atmosphere with ash, and lowering the Earth's temperature for a number of years thereafter. It also produced brilliant sunrises, maybe like this one that we witnessed over the Indian Ocean.

A brilliant sunrise near Krakatoa.

Side Note: On December 22, 2018 a tsunami caused by the eruption of Anak Krakatau, or Child of Krakatoa, created a landslide underwater on the volcano's slope, displacing a large volume of water that slammed into the islands of Java and Sumatra killing more than 400 people. Anak Krakatau, also in the Sunda Strait is one of the most active volcanoes in the world.

The voyage took 30 days, which included a single stop for 4 days in Cape Town, South Africa. I was on my way to circumnavigating the world by traveling in a westerly direction the entire way.

Crossing the Equator

A fire hose whipping, and into the cage we went.

The *FDR* crossed the equator and entered the domain of King Neptune Rex where an ancient ceremony took place. The crew was divided into two groups—those who had crossed the equator before (*shellbacks*) and those who had not (*pollywogs*). The shellbacks imposed a reign of terror over the pollywogs, initiating them with various hazing rituals into the domain of *King Neptune Rex*, sovereign ruler of the Raging Main. For example, we pollywogs were required to stand watch to look for mail buoys, chase snipe, eat seaweed (spinach and pepper), crawl through chutes filled with a slurry of garbage and bilge water, withstand the force of high-pressure fire hoses, endure beatings. Finally, after all of that, we were admitted to King Neptune's Court.

Running the gauntlet.

A slurry of garbage and bilge water.

The King's Court

Entering the King's Court was, by far, the worst part of the whole experience. Sitting on a throne was the *king* with his henchmen sitting in a circle before him—they were seven of the fattest men on the ship and their bellies were covered with axel grease. Before long, we pollywogs would be kissing those bellies having grease smeared all over our faces and hair. Not only did our pride suffer, our bodies did as well. I was not unscathed.

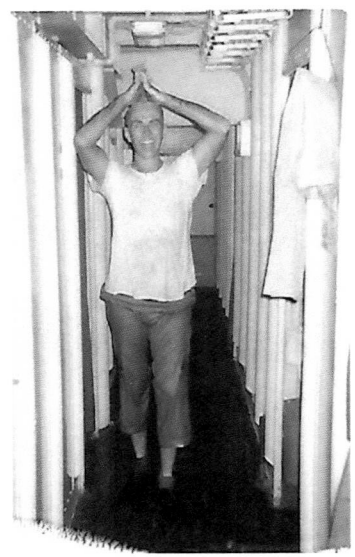

Greasy hair after being admitted to King Neptune's Court.

Once the ceremony was over, I got out my razor and became a skinhead for a while; no detergent onboard could remove that grease. But, for all that, we had now morphed from pollywogs into shellbacks. My proudest Navy memorabilia, the one that hangs over my desk to this day, is my framed shellback certificate.

Port Call in Cape Town, South Africa

The South Africans greeted us with an outpouring of curiosity and goodwill. However, because of apartheid, we were not permitted ashore. The black sailors (about 400) aboard would not have been treated well. Over a 4-day period, a vast number of visitors (estimated to be 100,000) crowded our decks from early morning to late in the afternoon to tour the ship. The following photograph depicts the onlookers as they crowded into the hanger bay.

Port call in Cape Town, South Africa.

As we approached the equator, traveling north off the west coast of Africa, the radioman in the radio shack was able to raise a ham radio operator in the states, and one at a time, we took turns talking to our families and loved ones that some of us had not seen, or even talked to, in nine months. The joy was apparent in our eyes as we completed those special calls. A few musicians organized a jam session and their uplifting tunes only added to the exuberance we felt.

A jam session on the voyage home.

A Sinuous Course

A long sea voyage was a time to unwind and decompress after months of stress and fatigue under combat conditions in a war zone. We had experienced our share of mishaps and accidents aboard ship, but now we worked on our tans and took life easy. I recall the navigator chiding the helmsman one day for steering a "sinuous course." It was readily apparent, watching the *Roosevelt's* wake that things had become just a little bit too loose aboard the ship.

Happy to Be Headed Home

I was happy to be headed home, we all were. I had many amazing memories, walking down streets in any number of Asian cities eagerly anticipating what I might see around the next corner or stumbling into a Buddhist temple in Hong Kong as I did once. Starting with my experiences in the Far East, I developed a deep appreciation of foreign cultures that has remained with me all my life. (Eventually, I would live in the Middle East for 4 months, which is another story of challenge and adventure to be told at another time.)

For now, though, we were headed home where the ship was scheduled for 6 months of overhaul and the crew for 6 months of leave. Upon reentering the Naval Station in Mayport, Florida, the *Roosevelt* was greeted by a modest crowd, mostly wives and children of the crew. (You can barely see the families on the pier in the photo below.)

Arrival home—Mayport, Florida.

The war in Vietnam was not popular and we felt it. We manned the rail, and when the gangplank was lowered, there were many tender moments as families reunited. Maybe in the eyes of our loved ones, we were heroes, then again, maybe not. It is hard to come to grips with that reality.

After a long deployment, all we wanted was to get off the ship and secure accommodations ashore. The married guys had wives and houses waiting for them. However, the government did not provide shore accommodations for us single officers. So, a group of us rented a house in Neptune Beach on Davis Street. We met and partied with a group of girls who had also rented a house on the beach. The social life was great. In fact, it was there that I met my future wife.

My motorcycle also landed in Mayport. The ship's crane lowered my Hong Kong prize to the pier. After uncrating and adding the appropriate fluids, the photo below is what she looked like, ready to ride. And I was ready to explore the Southeast on my brand-new Honda motorcycle. The only alteration I made was to raise the handlebars.

My motorcycle on the pier in Mayport.

On one occasion when I was riding along next to the St. Mary's River on the border of Florida and Georgia, I had a flat tire. It was the front wheel, so I was able to take it off and I hitched a ride to the Jacksonville bus terminal where I called Ron Van Allen, a fellow junior officer on the ship, who came and picked me up—Thanks, Ron.

Alongside an oiler.

Emergency Breakaway

After two 30-day leave periods, one for each half of the crew, we operated in the Atlantic on and off for another 6 months with a full crew. While at sea during this time, the ship was alongside an oiler taking on black oil, jet fuel, and aviation gasoline. The fuel was being pumped over through hoses that hung from span wires, which were attached at either end between the two ships. Suddenly, the oiler lost its steering and her stern started swinging in our direction, to port. *There was going to be a collision in a matter of seconds.* The refueling detail reacted immediately, scrambling they disconnected the hose fittings as we prepared for an emergency breakaway. Oil had spilled on the sponson decks, and there were two men in the water, which was cascading between the ships. The sailors had lost their footing and slipped overboard.

On the navigation bridge, the helmsman quickly altered course to starboard and we arrived at a course that roughly paralleled the oiler for a few seconds. The impending collision was avoided. As the two ships moved farther apart, the span wires stretched tight and then began to pop.

Rescued by Helicopter

The men in the water were picked up by our rescue helicopter (we carried two Sea Sprite helicopters on board), which had its rotor blades in motion, prepared for just this type of incident. I ran up to the flight deck and watched as the Executive Officer met the two men who had been in the water. One of the men was Howard Dyer, a friend and a junior officer from engineering. They were both OK. Now when we get together at the annual *FDR* reunions, I always enjoy hearing Howard recount the event with the same enthusiasm, as if it had just happened yesterday.

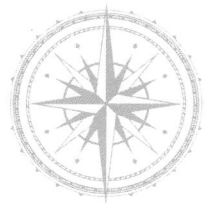

CHAPTER 6

Some White-Knuckle Flying and Russian Interference at Sea

First Stop—Guantanamo Bay, Cuba

I t was 0500 on the first morning of our Operational Readiness Inspection at Guantanamo Bay, Cuba (August 1967). I was at my watch station on the Special Sea and Anchor Detail. It was our duty to get the ship underway every day at this time, long before the rest of the crew was awake, steaming through the channel and out to sea to begin flight operations. With the exception of Officer Candidate School, this was the most intensive training I ever had in a multitude of skills, chief among them—damage control.

Guantanamo Bay is located on the south side of Cuba. That week, the northerly winds were light as we cruised south to gain sea room, and then north to make enough wind across the deck to launch our planes. Without enough wind, they cannot get airborne. The pilots were becoming accustomed to operating off the flight deck of a carrier once again. Launch and recovery took a long time and the carrier was covering quite a bit of water in the direction of the shore. It was important that there was enough time to regain sea room before the next launch and recovery cycle!

Operating off the coast of Guantanamo Bay, Cuba.

All day long we would launch and recover, losing sea room every cycle. Finally, we had to miss a cycle in order to get far enough out to sea to avoid running into shallow water. That's why the training is called an *inspection*—so that these types of problems are uncovered. I understood the reason for the intensity of the training, coming as it did, only a month after the catastrophic fire on the USS *Forrestal* in which nearly 200 sailors lost their lives. (That story is told in the book, *Sailors to the End: The Deadly Fire on the USS* Forrestal *and the Heroes Who Fought It* by Gregory A. Freeman.)

Returning to port every day in the late afternoon, we were given time to go ashore. I spoke to some Cuban workers who lived off-base in Cuba proper. These were times of tension between Castro's Cuba and the United States, but the Cubans were happy to be working on the base for good wages.

My fellow officers and I spent time at the Officers Club, where I also enjoyed playing tennis. One day, I rented a small sailboat—an O'Day Cape Cod Bulls Eye—and navigated the waters of Guantanamo Bay. I sailed under the stern of the great carrier that I called home and ventured far too close to the shores that belonged to Fidel Castro. Sunset in August came late, and I explored much of the shoreline of Guantanamo Bay by myself and at my leisure. Besides the Special Sea and Anchor Detail, I was part of a Damage Control Station where we were drilled, tested and evaluated on how to fight disasters at sea. We learned a lot from the inspectors who instructed us and then evaluated us on how well we could execute the drill. The whole process was very intense.

Supersonic in an F4 Phantom

Long before we left the states for the Mediterranean Sea in August of 1967, I jumped at the chance to take a 2-day course at Cecil Field near Jacksonville, on how to survive in a high-performance jet fighter. I certified to fly in the back seat—air sickness, low-pressure breathing, ejection seat practice, and so on. I strapped myself into the Martin-Baker ejection seat, pulled the curtain, and was ejected by the force of an explosive charge, up a metal pole about 10 feet into the air, seat and all. In the low-pressure chamber, we reached an air pressure equivalent of 35,000 feet where our reaction and judgment capability were tested. There were lectures on the effects of low air pressure on the brain and other topics. I filed away my completion certificate until we were well into our Med cruise where I could put it to good use.

The plane I flew with LCDR Aucoin, the F-4 Phantom II.

Months later, I inquired among the squadrons of Carrier Air Wing 1 embarked aboard the *Roosevelt* and finally found a pilot, Lieutenant Commander (LCDR) James B. Aucoin, in Fighter Squadron VF-32 who was willing to take me on a hop. His Radar Intercept Officer (RIO) the person that sits in the seat behind the pilot was sick with a head cold and was unable to fly. (Think

Maverick and Goose in the movie *Top Gun*.) The RIO was about my size and his G-suit fit me fine. He willingly covered the basics of what I might be required to do once in the air.

The next morning, I was in the ready room (just a little tense) with the pilots and RIOs flying in that sortie. Soon we were strapped into our seats, waiting to proceed to the catapult. The combination of wind speed, ship speed, the F-4 afterburners, and the push from the catapult would get us to an airspeed of 130 miles per hour in just a few ticks of the second hand of my watch. That's the airspeed we needed to fly. When the launch occurred, the papers I had on a clipboard on my right knee were all over the cockpit. The squadron Commanding Officer (CO) had briefed us that we would be flying a practice bombing mission over a pile of rocks in the ocean off the coast of Spain.

We approached the target straight on and leveled out at 15,000 feet of altitude. Then, LCDR Aucoin flipped the plane upside down and pulled back on the stick that normally sends the plane upward, but because we were upside down, the plane took a downward turn. I looked up through the canopy only to see the ocean over my head. He then flipped the plane right side up, held it for a moment, and released the first practice bomb. He pulled back on the stick again to pull the plane out of its steep dive. We leveled out at about 1,000 feet. It felt to me like we were barely skimming the water. Then, we left the target area. We had just dive-bombed; this maneuver was called a "Split S." (The Split S is an air combat maneuver.) Over the headset, Aucoin asked me if the bomb delivered on target.

I answered "I don't know, I didn't really see it."

"OK" he said, "let's try it again." We did it again and I started to catch on. By the third time, the bomb was right on target and I saw it very well. Talk about "white-knuckle" flying, this was it. We headed back to the ship. I am fairly sure that the rocks in the photograph below are the ones off the coast of Spain that we used for target practice that day—but it's hard to tell—everything was in such a whirl.

Target practice bombing mission off the coast of Spain.

We Go Supersonic

On our return flight to the ship, LCDR Aucoin asked if I would like to go supersonic.

"Yes," I replied mixing with the excitement of the moment with the danger of, well, the same moment. He hit the afterburners and I watched as the Mach meter crept up to 1.0 and then on up to 1.1. We did it! While those outside the plane may have heard a sonic boom, I heard nothing at all inside the rear seat of the cockpit. Returning to subsonic speed, we approached the ship.

It was now time to make one of those race-track-type landings followed by a controlled crash, as the Phantom caught one of the four wires stretched across the deck. I couldn't tell which one we caught. In an optimal landing, the pilot will catch the number 2 wire with the jet's tailhook. Oh, and just before the wheels of the plane hit the deck, the pilot pushes the engine to full power. The wire, if you catch it, tries to stop the plane and the engines try to accelerate it at the same time. To an observer, it's a war of opposing forces that produces a giant screeching sound loud enough to deafen a person. Because of the force of the impact of an arrested landing, it is past time for the guy in the back seat to "duck and cover." The pilot, of course, has to endure the same impact with his eyes open, it is hoped. The flight deck personnel wear noise attenuators although I'm not sure how they could block out that much noise! The full-power part of the landing ensures that the plane can get airborne again if it fails to catch a wire—a "no-no," but it does happen—it's what's called a "bolter." After three of those, the pilot must refuel (midair) and head for the closest land. For the *Roosevelt* on station in the Med, the "bingo" field as they referred to it was Sigonella on the island of Sicily.

An Air Show at Sea

CDR Max Barr wraps his A-4 around the superstructure.

Throughout my 2 years aboard the *Roosevelt*, I never tired of watching air operations. About an hour before my bridge watch, I would often go up to the 08 level (8 decks above the main deck) on the island, find a good place to perch, and then just watch the planes, each trying to do the same thing successfully: launch and recover. From the smallest, the A4 Skyhawk that John McCain flew off the *Oriskany* and the *Forrestal*, to the largest, the A3 Skywarrior which launched at 73,000 pounds, each type of plane had its own challenges. Deploying to the Mediterranean in 1967–1968 was decidedly "down-tempo" compared to the Tonkin Gulf. And that gave our air wing time to prepare and put on an air show for visiting dignitaries and, of course, for any of the crew who cared to watch. What a show to see!

At the Air Show, everyone was in rapt attention.

In one maneuver, Commander Max Barr, Commander, Carrier Air Wing 1, appeared to wrap his little A4 Skyhawk around our superstructure. He made his plane do all it could do just about standing it on the edge of its wing. Everybody was in rapt attention. In another maneuver an F8U Crusader flew up our port beam and released a parachute flare in the air just ahead of the *Roosevelt*. Then another plane came over the horizon from the starboard bow and launched a sidewinder missile that made a bull's-eye strike on the parachute flare. No wonder air power is considered so decisive in warfare at sea.

A Hair-Raising Landing

In addition to flying ashore ahead of each port call to set up land tours (my new job in the Med), I had one other opportunity to fly jets in the Mediterranean—this time it was in a Navy T-33 jet trainer—when the *Roosevelt* was anchored in Barcelona Harbor. The catapult officer on the *Roosevelt*, LCDR Dale DeWeese, an aviator I knew in the Air Department, needed some flight time to maintain his flying status. He asked me to accompany him and, of course, I said yes.

T-33 Jet Trainer

Dale Logs Some Flight Time

We went to Barcelona International Airport, checked out a plane and strapped in for the flight. I was a passenger in the rear seat. (In the photo above, Dale is standing on the wing and I am on the ground.) As always, I had my camera. I got some pretty good shots including one of the *Roosevelt* anchored in the harbor.

After our time aloft, Dale radioed the tower for landing instructions. I could hear the reply he received on the radio—"Wait."

Another request from Dale, and another reply, "Wait." Precious time was slipping away.

Finally, with urgency, Dale said, "Request landing instructions, our fuel state is critical." No response.

After a prolonged delay, Dale informed me that we were "going in." This sounded a little unorthodox from Dale who was a very level-headed guy that I knew fairly well. It was then, I realized that this was a real emergency, and something had to be done. That said, Dale headed for the runway and started our approach.

What was the problem with the tower? The fact was that after this long delay, we had less than 40 gallons of gas left in the tanks (two wing tip tanks)—and we *had to land!* To make matters worse, we were getting no assistance from the tower. We heard plenty of Spanish being spoken on the other end of the radio, but no English.

As we approached the airport, we saw a small plane taxiing onto the runway ahead of us from the left. We were rapidly closing in on him and something "bad" was about to happen. At the last moment, Dale pulled the jet into a steep left bank, which allowed the small plane to pick up speed and take off. After that left bank turn, we came around, straightened out and landed well behind the small plane, which thankfully was already in the air. The fuel tanks were almost dry when we landed. Dale parked the plane, and we exited through the terminal without "waiting for instructions." As far as I know, nothing more ever came of it. It was one of the most totally unexpected and dangerous events in my life!

Russian Warships in the Mediterranean

During the Cold War (1947–1991), the USSR challenged the United States worldwide. Nowhere was that challenge more evident than at sea. The *Roosevelt* had already faced Russian ships in the Tonkin Gulf (see Chapter 4). Now, in the Mediterranean, we faced them again. These ships provided visual confirmation of the Russian challenge, and thus, the purpose of our mission.

Russian warship in the Mediterranean Sea.

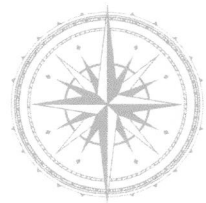

CHAPTER 7

A New Job in the Mediterranean and an SOS

Our sailors investigate the Parthenon in Athens, Greece.

My new billet (job responsibility) on this deployment (1967-'68) was Special Services. A few days before arriving at our next port of call, as mentioned earlier I would fly ashore aboard the Carrier Onboard Delivery (COD) aircraft (mail plane) in order to set up tours for the crew. I would meet with prospective tour operators, listen to their pitches, and then select the one that I thought our crew would most appreciate. Accepting gifts from any of the tour operators was a definite rule breaker. In Piraeus, Greece (port city of Athens), one tour operator offered me a small bag of pine nuts. Little did I know then that my future wife of 22 years would use *snauba* (pine nuts) to cook the most delicious *kibbeh* (a Lebanese dish made of bulgur wheat, minced onions, finely ground lamb plus spices) I have ever tasted, or that I would enjoy them again when I lived in the Middle East in Amman, Jordan in 2000–2001.

Over the course of the 9-month cruise, about half of our time was spent steaming at sea and the other half either riding at anchor or in port. When riding at anchor in some remote bay, the ship did not burn fuel, nor did we have liberty. For example, we spent 3 days at anchor in Suda Bay on the Greek island of Crete, where I enjoyed some of the largest and most delicious oranges I have ever tasted. On another occasion, we enjoyed "swim call" while at anchor in Augusta Bay, Sicily. In Barcelona, Spain, Biff Brotherton USMC and I caught a bus to the country of Andorra high in the Pyrenees Mountains on the border of Spain and France. It is famous for its wine and postage stamps. Biff and I are standing next to wine barrels in Andorra.

Biff Brotherton and I travel to Andorra high in the Pyrenees.

One of the most offbeat liberty ports we visited was Taranto, Italy. We dropped anchor in the harbor on Halloween—October 31, 1967, and stayed for 7 days, which gave us plenty of time to visit the grand nineteenth-century piazzas. Taranto, a classic old Italian city, is located on the underside of the arch of the Italian boot and at that time, was not often visited by American sailors.

Valletta, Malta

We made two port calls to the island country of Malta, both during the winter. On November 20, 1967, we "dropped the hook" about a mile from the pier in the harbor at Valletta. The personnel boats (which carry about 80 people) were lowered over the side and when "liberty" was piped, there were 1,300 *Roosevelt* sailors poised to go ashore, including myself.

A few hours after we dropped the anchor and all 1,300 men were ashore, the wind picked up and with it, the waves began to build. Boating was canceled and we were stranded ashore for what ended up being 4 days. Four of us junior officers made it to the Royal Air Force air base where we found lodging in a Quonset hut. However, there was no heat in late November, and none of us were prepared to "rough it" for 4 days. The 1,300 sailors found lodging where they could, and some had to spend the night out in the November cold.

The *Roosevelt* had two Sea Sprite helicopters aboard, so the next day one was readied with the pilot, a disbursing clerk, and a bag of money in the back. A pay line was opened onshore so that the sailors could get paid. At that point, the crew could afford lodging and necessities. We left Malta on the November 26th. The next port of call was Marseille, France on December 4th.

My parents and my sister, Judy, visit me in Cannes, France.

My Family Comes to Visit

We pulled into Cannes, France just in time to celebrate Christmas. My mother had never traveled outside the United States. My father had been to Europe on the school ship at the New York State Merchant Marine Academy in 1924. I sent money home for three airplane tickets so that my parents and sister could fly over and visit me on the ship in Cannes for Christmas 1967. After Cannes, they traveled to Paris to take in some sights. Then, a few days later I took leave and joined them in Paris. Among the highlights was Notre Dame Cathedral seen in 1966.

Notre Dame Cathedral (Monday, April 15, 2019)

On April 15, 2019, a fire broke out in the attic of the cathedral. It quickly spread to the timbers and the 250 tons of lead that supported the spire. (Note the spire between the two towers in the photo of the church.) As the spire toppled, the sky lit up orange as flames shot out of the roof behind the nave of the cathedral. Initial reports stated that the fire was halted, and damage was limited. Many artifacts were lost but many were saved.

Notre Dame Cathedral and its famous spire (between the two towers).

For centuries, Notre Dame has been and continues to be one of the most visited landmarks in the world. It is 850 years old. We managed to get to Ile de la Citi, an island on the Seine River where the cathedral is located where we saw the gargoyles and the flying buttresses.

The exquisite stained glass rose windows within Notre Dame.

We saw the exquisite stained glass rose windows. It is reported that the windows appear to be intact but are probably suffering "thermal shock" from the intense heat on the fire followed by cold water. This means that the glass, set in lead, may have sagged or been weakened. The windows are reputed to be priceless.

Restoring the cathedral will take time and money. Fortunately, Notre Dame is a thoroughly documented building. Over the years, historians and archeologists have made extensive plans and images, including minutely detailed 3-D laser-scanned recreations of the interior. Once the building is stabilized and the damage assessed, restoration work can begin. However, just a few days after the fire, I saw reports of people rioting against restoration because they think that the donated billion dollars should go to them.

Some of my duties as Special Services Officer

On our second visit to Malta (January 22) as part of Special Services Officer duties, I organized a dance at a private club in the countryside. I called around to find and invite women's organizations to attend. The British Wrens arrived on a bus as well as other invited guests. Many thanks to Biff Brotherton, my tough Marine friend from Walla Walla, Washington, who lived in our passageway on the ship, for helping me to shut down the party and send the lingerers on their way. I am sad to say that Biff, who had such a dynamic personality, has since passed. In addition to being a good friend, we also traveled together around the Mediterranean.

Our most frequent port of call was Naples, Italy. Another one of my duties as Special Services Officer was coaching the ship's basketball team. The *Roosevelt's* team was entered in a holiday basketball tournament at the Naval Support Activity, Bagnoli, outside of Naples. It was my job as the coach to also setup travel for the team to the tournament. At the time, the *Roosevelt* was operating in the Tyrrhenian Sea off the coast of Italy near Rome. We lowered one of our personnel boats over the side, boarded the basketball team and headed for Rome which is on the Tiber River. (Rome has no deep-water port of its own, so we had to run one of our liberty boats in.) There, we boarded our bus and started to drive through the streets of Rome.

Holiday basketball tournament, Bagnoli, Naples, Italy.

The Pope's Weekly Address

The Pope making his weekly address from the Papal residence.

As we drove along, I realized that we were near the Vatican. I also knew that the Pope (Pope Paul VI) was due to make his weekly Papal Address from his residence, the balcony overlooking St. Peter's Square. And amazingly, it was close to the time of the weekly address—I couldn't believe that our timing was so perfect. As senior officer aboard the bus, I told the driver to drive to St. Peter's Square, pull up close and stop the bus. We waited about 20 minutes, and then the Pope appeared and spoke to the crowd. From there we drove on to the tournament in Naples.

(Nineteen years later, as a member of the Naval Reserves, I was mobilized for the Libyan strike in April 1986, and was detailed to go to the Naval Support Activity [NSA] in Bagnoli. I expand on this in Chapter 8.)

In addition to arranging shore tours and coaching the basketball team, I also edited the ship's newsletter. I spent long hours with Executive Officer (XO) Captain von Schrader, putting the finishing touches on the document before going to press. He was a highly decorated pilot and, also an intellectual. After his tour aboard the *Roosevelt*, he was assigned to the Chief of Naval Operations staff and later became a Fellow at the Brookings Institute. He was a very capable leader.

An SOS from One of Our Destroyers ... Roosevelt to the Rescue

Photo # KN-16237   USS Bache aground off Rhodes, Greece, 1968

We lose a destroyer at anchor in the harbor on the Island of Rhodes.

One day (February 6, 1968) while anchored in Suda Bay, Crete, we received a distress call from the USS *Bache* (DD-470), an American destroyer at anchor in the harbor on the Greek island of Rhodes off the coast of Turkey. The *Roosevelt* got underway to render assistance. We arrived the next morning to find that a sudden storm with high winds and waves that rose to more than 16 feet had driven the *Bache* onto the rocks. The *Bache*'s anchor did not hold and the two boilers they had on-line were not enough to save the ship from running aground on the rocks.

Most of the 230-odd crew members on the destroyer had managed to make it to shore, leaving only the commanding officer and 29 crewmen behind. These courageous men elected to remain onboard in an effort to shore up the stricken vessel and prevent further damage. They worked throughout the night in darkness punctured only by occasional battle lanterns. The hull had been torn from stem to stern, she was leaking badly, most of her main mast was gone, and she had lost all electrical power. Her only means of communication was by battery-powered flashing lights. Miraculously, there were no casualties, but the ship was a total loss on the rocks of that harbor.

We Lend Assistance

The *Roosevelt*'s Damage Control Assistant and an EOD (Explosive Ordinance Demolition) team were immediately dispatched to the ship to estimate the amount damage and lend assistance to the remaining destroyer crewmen. Throughout the day, the *Roosevelt* remained on the scene assisting in the rescue efforts. We continuously shuttled food and clothing to the *Bache* crewmen, both those ashore and those onboard the damaged ship. All small arms aboard the *Bache* were transferred to the *Roosevelt* for safekeeping, as well as the Disbursing Officer's cash and vouchers. *Roosevelt* signalmen remained on station to monitor and relay messages sent from the destroyer.

Shortly before the *Roosevelt* got underway again, Rear Admiral V.G. Lambert, Commander Carrier Division Six was relieved of his rescue coordination duties by Rear Admiral Isaac C. Kidd and his assistants who had been sent to evaluate the damage, investigate the cause of the mishap, and direct salvage operations.

Once again, the *Roosevelt* was underway to her next port of call—our crew was saddened at the loss of a naval ship, but thankful that no lives had been sacrificed—and glad that we were able to provide assistance to the destroyer's crew.

Lava from Mt. Etna

Steaming along the coast of Sicily one night, we observed molten lava flowing down the side of Mt. Etna, an active volcano at the time. Almost 30 years later, my wife and I took a cruise around the Hawaiian Islands in 1996 where we saw molten lava from the Kilauea volcano running down the side of the volcano all the way to the sea where it burst into giant clouds of steam. This process produced the black granules of sand that covered the beaches there. The sand was made instantaneously by the sudden mixing of the hot lava and cold seawater and not by the mechanical action of wind and water over decades. I didn't know that!

Spit and Polish and Change of Command

The time we spent at anchor in the Mediterranean left plenty of opportunity for formal inspections. In the photo below you can see that "spit and polish" was the order of the day.

In the Mediterranean there was plenty of time for formal inspections.

There were also "Change of Command" ceremonies, where the crew welcomed visiting dignitaries such as ambassadors, a consul general, the Belgian Minister of Defense, as well as admirals, generals, and mayors. All of this was very formal. At the change of command, the crew welcomed our new skipper, Captain Gordon Hodgson (see the cake in the photo).

The change of command ceremony while in Valencia.

We arrived in Valencia, Spain on March 14, just in time to participate in Valencia's annual Fallas Festival, one of the largest and best-known festivals in Europe. Nightly international competitive fireworks displays, bullfights, and rubbing shoulders with more than one million European tourists made this port one of our most exciting ports of call. I flew into port a day or two early to interview tour operators and select tours the sailors. Many of the sailors took advantage of the ship-sponsored tours to Madrid and Toledo, Spain.

The Fallas Festival, one of the largest and best-known festivals in Europe.

On March 29th, we were in Genoa for an 8-day visit. Again, I flew in early to set up tours, this time I booked 2- or 3-day tours to Pisa, Venice, Florence, and Munich. After one of the Venice tours, there was a close call—the bus had been delayed, and the sailors made it back just before the ship set sail. For centuries Genoa rivaled Venice as an important Italian sea power, trading city, and financial center. Genoa claims Christopher Columbus as their native son.

We had one last liberty port to visit before heading for home. Palma Mallorca was a garden spot in the Mediterranean and it was springtime in May—the weather was perfect. We enjoyed ourselves as did the many Swedes who also vacationed there. I participated in a wine tasting as seen in the photograph below—the wine was exceptional. Have you ever joined in a wine tasting like this one?

Wine tasting in Mallorca.

Palma was famous for its Mallorca pearls, an oyster pearl developed by a process peculiar only to this area. There were many beautiful beaches around the periphery of the island, and wonderful sightseeing opportunities in the villages inland.

The *Roosevelt* pulled into Pollenca Bay, also located on the island of Mallorca, to rendezvous with the USS *Independence* (CVA-62) which was there to relieve us. We spent a day with our counterparts on the *Independence* briefing them on what to expect in the Mediterranean. It was a standard practice aboard ship for any watch stander to brief his relief on what the current situation was and what to expect in the near future. So, collectively, the *Roosevelt* crew briefed the crew of the *Independence* and our responsibility passed.

The Strait of Gibraltar

After the long deployment (9 months) to the Mediterranean Sea, the ship transited the Strait of Gibraltar and headed for home across the Atlantic. I was standing the mid-watch (midnight to 4:00 am) on the bridge as we passed through the straits and recall the anemometer (wind gauge) reading a steady 60 knots of headwind for the entire watch, 4 hours straight! We left behind an endurance record: No U.S. aircraft carrier had spent more time on station in the Mediterranean than the *Roosevelt*. We helped keep the peace.

Skeet Shooting off the Fantail

As Special Services Officer, I arranged for skeet shooting off the fantail of the ship while we were at sea. Shotguns were brought up from the armory including mine, an over-under double-barreled shotgun I purchased in a port in the Med. We broke out the ammunition—thousands of rounds of shotgun shells I purchased at a recommended gun shop several ports before. The shooter, standing at the ready, would take aim, give the command "pull" and start tracking the trajectory of the clay pigeon with the barrel of his shotgun. The clay pigeon was hand-launched. The idea was that the shooter would (hopefully) blast the skeet right out of the air. Each man got five shots and then passed the shotgun to the next. It was great fun.

Skeet shooting off the fantail.

Footnote: Skeet shooting is popular aboard Navy ships. The advent of air power as a weapon at sea changed everything. A swarm of enemy aircraft (even before kamikaze) might penetrate close aboard trying to deliver a bomb right on the flight deck or a torpedo just below the waterline. It soon became apparent that aircraft carriers, indeed every ship in the Navy, needed more "ack-ack" (close in, rapid fire) antiaircraft weaponry. And Navy gunners needed to be trained to aim high and lead the target. Skeet shooting was just one of the training exercises the Navy used to provide that training. In the mid-1950s, when the Roosevelt went into the yards to be modified by adding an angle flight deck, eight of her 5" 54 caliber gun mounts were removed and close in, rapid fire antiaircraft weaponry was added in their place to knock down enemy planes that had penetrated close in. Big guns on Navy warships had become a thing of the past.

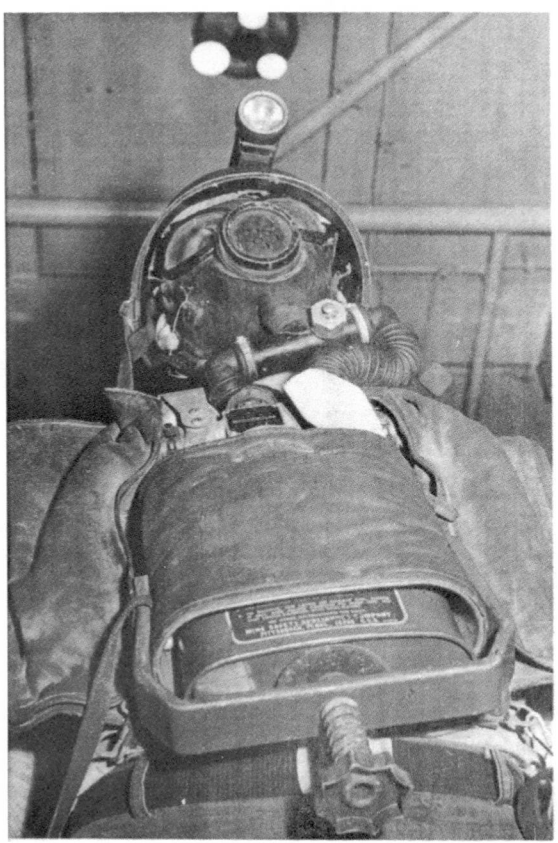

Oxygen Breathing Apparatus mannequin on the mess deck.

Horseplay on the Voyage Home

Ever mindful of safety at sea, a mannequin was set up on the mess deck wearing an Oxygen Breathing Apparatus (OBA) as an example to the crew in case of fire. After a few days, it went missing. There was an air of horseplay about the mess deck. Later, we heard the bosun's mate piping, "Man overboard, now all hands, muster on station." I hustled up to my muster station where they took a headcount of all assigned personnel and reported: "All present or accounted for." The lookout had reported a *man overboard*. After an hour or so of searching, we resumed our westerly course. It was horseplay, but the incident was not forgotten. Because of the horseplay our arrival back in homeport, originally scheduled for Sunday, May 19, 1968, was delayed by 2 days,

A New Homeport and an Overhaul

Upon arrival in Mayport, Florida, the *FDR* tied up at the pier for about 60 days to give the crew time to go on liberty and to see their families. With half the crew on leave, the *FDR* was in a period of Restricted Availability. After that, we got underway and steamed for Portsmouth Naval Shipyard, Virginia for an extended overhaul that would last 2 years. *FDR* was there for one last modernization, which would allow the A-6 Intruder and the A-7 Corsair aircraft the ability to fly until 1977, when she would be scrapped. Our new homeport for that period of time was Norfolk, Virginia.

We loaded many hundreds of our dependents' cars onto the hanger deck and the flight deck in preparation for the move. I was on deck early on the morning of our departure.

Dependents' cars were loaded for the permanent move to Norfolk.

And there on the pier was my girlfriend, Madeleine, and her sister, Paula, to wave "goodbye" to me.

Discharge and Promotion

Within a month or two of arriving at Norfolk, I was discharged with 4 years of active duty and the rank of Lieutenant (O-3). I had recently made O-3 in slightly less than 4 years. Accelerated promotion during wartime was not uncommon.

I was discharged in Norfolk as an O-3 (Lieutenant) with almost 4 years of service.

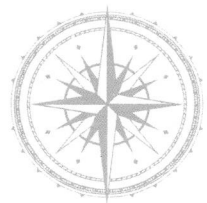

CHAPTER 8

A Citizen Sailor (1968–1987) and the Libyan Call Up

I left the Navy in 1968 to pursue an MBA degree at the Wharton School at the University of Pennsylvania in Philadelphia. I packed my belongings into a wooden sea chest that was made for me in the carpenter shop aboard the *Roosevelt*. I sold my motorcycle and turned it over to the buyer the day I left the ship. A buddy then drove me to the Greyhound bus station. I was shedding a lot of my recent past when I stepped off the gangplank of that ship—now in dry dock at Portsmouth Naval Shipyard. I was on my way to Philadelphia—I was a military veteran going back to college like so many of my contemporaries. And we were returning to a college atmosphere the likes of which we had never seen before. Demonstrations were loud and sometimes violent. The military, and especially men in uniform, were targeted and despised as "baby killers."

While still stationed at Mayport Naval Station, Florida, I met my future wife and the mother of my three sons. She was from a fine family in Jacksonville, Florida. Madeleine knew that I *only* drove a motorcycle. But her parents did not. When I showed up to meet them before my first date with Madeleine, they tried not to act too shocked to see my motorcycle in their driveway. I was quickly, but tactfully, informed that Madeleine would not be riding on the back of any motorcycle, but that she and I were welcome to take her car on the date. By March of 1969 we were married.

Madeleine and I begin dating long distance between Jacksonville and Norfolk.

Joining the Navy Reserves

The GI Bill was paying my tuition and we were living in married student housing at the University of Pennsylvania. For about a year and a half, I went to school and never once thought about any continuing affiliation with the Navy. That was behind me. But, in spite of the GI Bill, I was running short of money. So, in order to make some additional income, I joined a unit of the Navy Reserves that was drilling at the Philadelphia Navy Yard. It was a one-night-a-week commitment and I actually enjoyed the night out with newfound Navy friends. Upon graduation from Penn, I joined IBM in Reading, Pennsylvania and began a career that took me to retirement in 1997.

Training Duty Aboard the USS **Trenton** (LPD-14) at Mardi Gras

In Reading, I continued drilling one night a week and 14 days once a year. I remember the two weeks of training duty I had in 1972 very well. I reported aboard the USS *Trenton* (LPD-14) for Mardi Gras in New Orleans. That's right, for Mardi Gras! The ship served as a floating hotel for ROTC units from across the South that were marching in the various Mardi Gras parades. The ship was tied up at the Louisa Street wharf along with the USS *Shreveport* (LPD-12), just a short walk from the French Quarter. Liberty went down every day at 1530 hours (3:30 pm). Not bad duty! When the week of fun was over, both ships got underway bound for Little Creek, Virginia where they were homeported.

We set the Special Sea and Anchor Detail and proceeded to make for open water. Eight hours and 125 miles later, we were in the open waters of the Gulf of Mexico, one of the longest Special Sea and Anchor Details I have ever stood on any ship. The Mississippi delta stretched out a long way into the Gulf from New Orleans, and of course, the only way for a ship to leave the delta was to follow the channel for 125 miles.

CIC Watch Officer aboard the USS *Trenton*, Gulf of Mexico.

We crossed the Gulf of Mexico, rounded Key West, and proceeded up the East Coast of Florida toward Cape Hatteras. There we ran into one of the worst storms I have ever encountered in the Atlantic. It was the only time I have ever been seasick aboard ship. I was standing the 8 to midnight watch as the CIC Watch Officer. The storm was so bad that we wedged ourselves in between pieces of equipment bolted to the floor so that we wouldn't be thrown from one side of CIC to the other. The mistake I made was to stop by the galley for a bite to eat before going on watch. The only food available was a pork sandwich, which I ate. After hours of the ship's rocking and pitching, I ran for the head and heaved everything out of my stomach. I went back and stood the rest of my watch feeling much relieved. Around 2345 (11:45 pm), the phone rang in CIC. It was my relief (and ship's company, I might add) saying that he was too sick to stand the midnight to 0400 (4:00 am) watch in CIC. I told him to go back to bed and I would stand his watch for him. During that watch, the lookouts reported losing a lifeboat over the side. Rifles were broken out of the armory to sink the lifeboat rather than have it wash ashore and possibly prompt a Coast Guard search for a ship that was actually safe in port.

A Hard Decision at the 13-Year Mark

In 1977, I transferred with IBM to Atlanta where I joined a team that had been assembled from across the country to develop packaged software for the manufacturing industry. These were System Engineers and Industry Specialists who really knew manufacturing and knew computers as well. I was honored to be counted among them. My hours were much more regular when I worked in the software lab than those when I called on customers in the field in Reading, Pennsylvania. But under Jimmy Carter, Naval Reserves strength was cut in half. *Being the new kid in the Navy Reserve Center in Atlanta*—we drilled on the Campus of Georgia Tech—*there was no pay billet for me* (the job responsibility I would hold within the unit). But they did allow me to put in my time for no pay. With 13 good years on the books, I decided I couldn't give up a weekend to drill for no pay. My time was worth something. It was more important to be home with my three boys. So, I dropped out of the Reserves for 2 years while I sorted things out.

A Lesson in Humility

Then one day two years later, I received a letter from the Navy saying that I had been placed on the Inactive Status List (ISL). It sounded horrible for someone like me who loved the service—so final, so wrong. I decided at that point to make my own future. I found a Sea Cadet Unit that drilled on the Campus of Georgia Tech once a week on Monday evenings. I then went to the non-pay unit I was supposed to be drilling with and asked them for temporary orders to the Sea Cadets. I taught the Sea Cadets weather forecasting, seamanship, rules of the road, things they would need to know when they got into the Navy, and more. It was a good compromise—my weekends were free for the family and I was able to maintain my relationship with the Navy, although still without pay. I did this for 6 months in 1980.

Picked Up by the Military Sealift Command

Then a big break came in the form of orders picking me up in a *pay status* with the Military Sealift Command (MSC). With these orders, it slowly dawned on me that for the last 2 years I had been learning a lesson in humility—that there was dignity in accepting that which I could not change. No amount of desire on my part could change the situation I was offered. When I had demonstrated that I accepted my fate, not giving up and walking away from the whole darned thing frustrated and mad—then things began to change for the better. I now look at it as a time of character building. You have character when you do what is right without anger and frustration, and without any guarantee of how it will turn out in the end.

By April 1986, I had completed the Military Sealift Command (MSC) curriculum (a series of two-week training courses once a year). MSC's mission was to move cargo for the Department of Defense (DOD). In times of peace there were regular shipping patterns. In times of emergency, Reserves were called up and extra ships were put into service to move vastly increased amounts of cargo to strategic hot spots.

We practiced by mobilizing our Reserve unit to the port of Savannah, Georgia, once a quarter. On one occasion, we participated in loading about 500 vehicles onto a RoRo ship, the USNS *Cygnus*, bound for a joint U.S./Egyptian military exercise. (A RoRo ship is a vehicle carrier ship.)

USNS *Cygnus* moving cargo for Military Sealift Command from Savannah to Egypt.

That weekend, the *Rainbow Warrior* was in port. In the photo, we are standing in front of the *Rainbow Warrior* on the pier in Savannah. The ship belongs to Green Peace, a nongovernmental organization (NGO) which supports a peaceful and sustainable world for future generations.

Our MSCO unit standing in front of the *Rainbow Warrior*.

Mobilized for the Libyan Strike

Demonstrators in Rome after the strike on Libya.

I was sitting at my desk at IBM in early April 1986 when the phone rang, and I was informed that I was being mobilized to …. they didn't/wouldn't even say where! I packed my bags and within a couple of days caught a plane from Atlanta to Naples, Italy, with several stops and plane changes. There were five of us reservists traveling there from MSC units across the country. (My four compatriots appear in the photo below.) We had been mobilized to run shipping exercises from ports in the U.S. to ports in the Mediterranean—one of those ports was Iskenderun, Turkey. We were located at Naval Support Activity, Bagnoli, outside of Naples (the same place where I had taken the ship's basketball team to play in a tournament 15 years earlier).

We were mobilized to Naval Support Activity, Bagnoli, Naples for the Libyan strike.

Every morning a squad of marines double-timed it around the inside perimeter of the NSA Compound in Bagnoli while calling a loud cadence. And every morning, traffic was blocked up at the gate while bomb detectors checked under every vehicle entering the station. A strange-looking guy appeared on the corner across from the main gate with a cart selling sunglasses. He was standing right in front of our hotel entrance and there was no one guarding our hotel. We called around on the phone for a less conspicuous hotel, but what we heard was "You American? No room for you." Air Force and Navy planes carried out the strike and Muammar Gaddafi was quieted for a long time.

After about two weeks of duty, the mission was complete. I took a long train ride from Naples to Frankfort, where I caught a plane home. The train ride covered about 1,400 miles with 2 overnights: Rome and Munich. When I arrived in Rome, I was greeted at the railroad station by a massive demonstration of Italian citizens protesting the air strike the United States had just delivered against Libya. They were probably not only demonstrating at the train station, but at key points across Rome and possibly across Italy. They appeared to be middle-class people, even families, waving Russian and Italian flags, animated but not hostile. (Fortunately, I was not in uniform at the time, because I was in travel status.) Being young and willing to take a chance at that stage of my life, I dared to discretely take photos of the demonstration.

The demonstrations continued.

Sweet Rewards

In my last eight years with the Military Sealift Command, I had the pleasure to meet some wonderful friends, including Bill Stoehs, the best man at my wedding to Cathy on June 1, 1996. (Madeleine and I divorced in June 1990.) Bill and his wife flew up from Florida to do the honors—they are still good friends.

Now that all the guys in the unit have retired from the Reserves, we get together maybe once a year for lunch at the Varsity in Atlanta to eat "dawgs," and tell sea stories. At this age, we know enough not to believe all of them. I have sailed the Atlantic, the Pacific, and the Indian Oceans in peacetime and in wartime. But what I really cherish are the friendships I have made along the way. I benefit from these friendships in a very real way, every day. The Navy has been very good to me.

Military Sealift Officers and their wives at the Navy Birthday Ball.

The Navy community in Atlanta was very active and Cathy and I enjoyed attending events such as the annual Navy Ball. In the above photograph are three MSC officers and their wives: Bill and Cathy, Dick and Joan, and Cathy and me at the Navy Ball in 1992. Cathy and I were dating at that time, hence the corsage, which Bill and Dick did not appreciate at all.

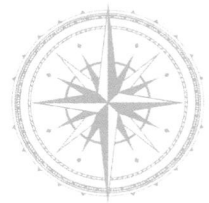

EPILOGUE:
After Retirement

Flying "Military Space Available"

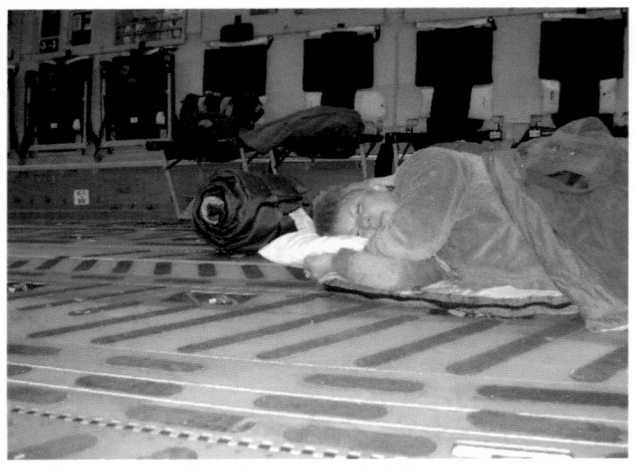

Cathy sleeping on the flight to Ramstein, Germany.

One of the most exciting aspects of being "retired military" is flying "military space available." On my first flight in March 2007, I took a hop from Charleston Air Force Base to Spangdahlem AFB, in Germany to try it out and see if I liked it. I also thought it might be a fun experience for Cathy since, as my dependent, she was qualified to fly with me. I flew on a C-17 cargo plane with the equipment it was transporting stowed and tied down in the center of the fuselage. Canvas seats lined the perimeter for passengers.

The number of passengers allowed on a flight depended on the amount of free space available after all the cargo was loaded. Cargo, of course, took top priority. On the negative side, any flight could be canceled at any time. And boarding a particular flight depended on the priority of those who signed up and those who were actually present in the terminal. I am retired military which means we are category VI, the lowest priority. To be successful at flying space available, a person needs to be flexible in both their time of departure and their destination! Otherwise, you return the next day and try again.

When Cathy and I took our first hop together in May 2008, I was thrilled that Cathy liked the experience, especially the convenience of unrolling a sleeping bag and stretching out on the cargo deck. She slept the entire long flight across the Atlantic to Germany. (The only rule we learned was that you may not sleep under the equipment.) One big advantage to flying military space available was the informal, no-hassle, environment in the passenger terminal—no long lines and no TSA. Other than that, a military passenger terminal pretty much functions like a commercial terminal, only with about 90 percent fewer passengers. And parking is free. Once I knew that we were confirmed on the flight, I called ahead for lodging in Germany to ensure we had a place to stay when we finally arrived the next day. The only expense associated with flying space available on a cargo plane was the nominal cost of a box lunch if you so desired.

We Explored the Rhine River

In Germany we took a short Rhine River cruise that included stops at Burg Reichenstein, Stephan's Wine Paradise, and the tourist town of Rudesheim. We also navigated the treacherous Lorelei where, through the ages, many ships have foundered on the rocks. We rode the cable car up the mountain commemorating the unification of Germany in 1871.

We visited the tourist town of Rudesheim.

The next year, in 2010, we took a hop to Travis AFB California where we toured Fisherman's Wharf in San Francisco and the wine country of Sonoma and Napa Valley, among other sights. We saw famous wineries including the Beringer mansion—note that the labels on the Beringer wine bottles show a picture of this mansion.

Among the famous vineyards we saw was the Beringer mansion.

Four travelers at Ramstein.

We returned to Germany in December 2012 to see the Christmas Markets with our space-available traveling friends, Mike and Kay. (Mike is retired Air Force.) The next morning, we sat with a German travel agent in the Ramstein Inn and booked our travel plans for the coming three weeks. After we planned our itinerary (it took three hours since we were going to see Christmas Markets in quite a few European cities), I asked the travel agent for a list of all the Gaffga families that lived in the area. There were about six. That was a surprise to me.

On my third phone call, I made a connection and we added a visit to St. Ingbert to visit Hans Jurgen Gaffga and his family. He was just my age and like me, he also had three sons. Here is his picture.

We met Hans Jurgen Gaffga, his wife, and family in St. Ingbert.

We witnessed the St. Wendeler Weihnachtsmarkt.

Notice the spelling of his last name on the name plate just above the doorbell—Gaffga— spelled the same as our name. I am confident in my knowledge of our family that our name has not been changed or shortened since our German ancestors came over from Germany. We took them out to dinner, and they took us to a Christmas Market, St. Wendeler Weihnachtsmarkt.

Notice in the photo below, the three wise men and their camels in the parade in St. Wendeler. There are also two scoundrels and two medieval storytellers in front of the camels. We felt the full measure of a European Christmas

Market experience during our visit to this town. A juggler, court jester as well as a live reindeer, sheep and other nativity animals completed the scene. We had a great one-day visit with the Gaffgas in St. Ingbert. Due to the language barrier, it was too difficult to discuss our genealogy, so we still don't know the family connection.

On another trip, we flew from Charleston AFB to March Air Reserve Base (ARB), rented a car and drove to Bakersfield, California, to visit friends. The four of us went to Santa Catalina Island off the coast of California. We saw bison and learned that several were imported from the states to provide background scenery for the filming of the Hollywood movie *The Plainsman*, many years ago. Now they roam free on Catalina Island. It was quite a tourist attraction.

In 2015, Cathy and I booked a repositioning cruise that embarked from Port Canaveral, crossed the Atlantic and made four ports calls before we debarked in Amsterdam. At the French port of Le Harve, we took an excursion to the beaches of Normandy and toured the cemeteries. What an unbelievable sacrifice our troops made in that invasion. (I have a cousin who died in Italy during the war; I guess we all have a relative who made the supreme sacrifice somewhere in that war.)

American cemetery at Normandy.

After four weeks of trekking through Holland, Belgium, and Germany in our group of four couples, two of the couples, us included, traveled to Ramstein AFB to catch a space available flight home.

Some of our hops have been to the West Coast, usually Travis AFB near Sacramento, March ARB near Los Angeles, or McChord AFB near Seattle. We even flew on a Navy C-130 from NAS Jacksonville bound for North Island near San Diego.

When flying to Europe, we can fly to Ramstein AFB Germany, Spangdahlem AFB Germany, or NAS Rota Spain. From these bases we can connect and fly to places farther away such as Hawaii or Alaska to the west or Mildenhall, United Kingdom, Aviano, Italy, or Sigonella or Sicily to the east. In all, we have taken more than a dozen vacations or about two dozen hops.

Cathy and I like the thrill of flying military space available never knowing for sure *when or where* the flights might take us. We also enjoy the fraternity of retired military people that we meet on these trips. I hope to take her to Guam one day, to see where I was stationed for a year and a half, and hopefully some of the other tropical islands of the South Pacific.

Cathy and I have also taken many ocean cruises. Recently, we took our first river cruise on the Danube. And we plan to do more river cruising in the future, perhaps in China. Even though military space available is the most challenging way to travel, it definitely has great rewards.

How to Fly "Military Space Available"

For those of you who are retired military, flying military can be a great benefit.

A good starting point is the Air Mobility Command website. <u>www.amc. af.mil/home/amc-travel-site/</u>.

Note: As mentioned above, flexibility is the key to flying military space available successfully. You need to be flexible on not only when you want to fly, but also where you want to go and when you need to return home. Being retired with no particular calendar obligations is ideal. Not owning pets is also desirable since you will most likely not be able to accurately predict your return home.

Step 1: Sign Up

About 60 days before you want to fly, send an email request to the base or bases you wish to fly out of. For example, on a recent hop from our home in South Carolina to the West Coast, I emailed a request to Charleston AFB and one to Jacksonville Naval Air Station, Florida. I allowed myself the flexibility to fly out of either base.

This 60-day time frame starts a 60-day clock ticking, which is used to establish your seniority on the flight—the lower your number, the higher your priority and higher your chance to get on the flight.

If you are planning a one- or two-week trip, it is a good idea to sign up for the return flight as well by submitting a space available request to the likely bases you might return from. Altogether, I might send email requests to 10 or 12 bases to cover my departure and return flights.

Step 2: Check the Flights

Now, you begin checking the official space available website for flights you might be interested in taking. The website address is: <www.amc.af.mil/home/amc-travel-site/>. The flights are listed by military terminal, departure day and time on a one- or two-day horizon. Each flight also lists the number of seats available: number firm and number tentative. I recommend checking flight availability a week or two before you want to fly.

Step 3: Show Up

When you have decided on your flight, pack your gear and travel to the base. For us, it will most likely be Charleston AFB, although we have also flown out of NAS Jacksonville and Dover AFB. The time listed for your flight is called "show time," and is usually two hours before takeoff. Drop your bags at the passenger terminal, park your car in long-term lot (free at Charleston AFB and NAS Jax). Then report to the desk and ask to be marked "present." All of this should be accomplished prior to *show time*.

A manifest will be posted, and you will be able to determine whether or not you are on the flight. If you are not manifested, you can stick around in case someone ahead of you on the list is a no-show. Remember, things are always changing. And if you discover that your flight is canceled, don't leave the terminal right away—it may reappear later as a scheduled flight.

Step 4: Make Reservations to Stay Over at Your Destination

Once confident that you will get on the flight, use a phone (AUTOVON) in the passenger terminal to make reservations to stay in Temporary Military Lodging (TML) when you arrive at your destination. For example, if you are flying overnight from Charleston AFB to Ramstein AFB in Germany, you will want to make a reservation not for the night you are flying, but for the next night. Accommodations at Ramstein AFB are excellent.

Step 5: Travel Arrangements at Your Destination

Due to the uncertain date/time of your arrival at your destination, you may want to sit down with a travel agent when you arrive at your destination. We have done this successfully with Ramstein Tour and Travel (RTT) located within the TML hotel located on the base across from the passenger terminal. They can help with everything from exotic excursions (to Paris, for example) to basic rail or bus transportation around Europe. They also publish a monthly newsletter with interesting excursions.

Working with the Sun City TV station, we developed a video on how to fly military space available, which can be viewed on YouTube. Go to <www.youtube. com> and search for "Lowcountry Snapshots." Then click on the photo of Cathy and me to see the video. (It is best to back up to the beginning of the video.)

A Shellback in Honolulu

As you can tell we like to travel and as mentioned, that includes ocean cruises as well as flying military space available. We took a Hawaiian cruise out of San Diego in 2010, which was delightful and relaxing. From the cruise port in

Honolulu we walked a short distance to Chinatown where we planned to eat dinner at a Chinese restaurant.

I noticed a tattoo shop a couple of doors down from the restaurant and suggested we take a look at their designs. "What are you thinking about doing?" Cathy wanted to know. "Surely you are not thinking of getting a tattoo, that's not something that my conservative husband would ever do. I am so sure you won't do it that I will pay for it if you do."

Without even thinking about it, I replied, that I had crossed the equator, been through the initiation process, and was duly certified as a *shellback* 42 years ago. It's probably time enough that I get the shellback tattoo. So, I decided to take Cathy up on her kind offer.

A *Shellback* in Honolulu.

The proprietor (the scary one in the photo below) had designs by Sailor Jerry, a pioneer in the tattoo business, designs that sailors like, and innovative inks he had developed for better, longer-lasting colors. I had never gotten a tattoo, never even had a mark on my body. This was a historic moment.

This tattoo parlor was an intimidating place—as creepy as the tattoo artist. The place was painted like a dungeon: gray walls with red paint splattered around to look like blood. The artist's girlfriend sat in a barber chair covered with some good-looking artwork around her midsection. Her chair was close enough to the wall to make the splattered paint look like a close shave gone wrong.

I climbed the stairs, and Cathy followed carrying the camera. She planned to take some really, good shots as the image of the *shellback* took shape on my butt. The guy said it wouldn't hurt, but, in reality it hurt like hell. Once the outline was completed, all that remained was to fill in the color, and finally it was done. At that point, I looked like a deer in the headlights (see the photo). We found an open drugstore and bought cream to apply for the next week on the voyage home. No sun and no swimming for a week or so.

It has held up well over the years; the lines and color are still crisp. The only inconvenience other than the needles was staying out of the sun and away from the shipboard pools on the way home. Not surprisingly, none of my three boys believed I really got a tattoo and I am not about to prove it, either!

The Roosevelt Reunion

In 1999, I discovered that there was a USS *FD Roosevelt* Reunion group that met on the same weekend every May in a different city each year. We go to these reunions unless there is a conflicting family obligation such as a graduation or a wedding.

Sometime around 2014, the *FDR* Reunion group commissioned and dedicated a monument to the *Roosevelt* on the Naval Base at Mayport, Florida, which was her homeport for most of her service life. In the photo, the little sailor in front is a caricature of President FD Roosevelt, who was a caricature himself.

The *Roosevelt* Reunion monument.

In May 2019, a joint reunion was held in San Diego for the three ships of the Midway class carriers: the USS *Midway*, the USS *Franklin D. Roosevelt*, and the USS *Coral Sea*. Called the "Three Sisters Reunion," it was perhaps the best reunion we've had thus far and included a banquet on the flight deck of the *Midway*.

The *Roosevelt* Reunion Reader.

Unfortunately, Pete Gutschneider, my roommate on the ship, was not well and could not attend. I am sad to have to report that he died on Memorial Day in 2019. He was a good friend and a good person to know. I knew him from the time I was assigned to work in Combat Information Center while on

Yankee Station off the coast of North Viet Nam. But it feels like I have known him much longer than that. He will be missed.

The Next Generation

When visiting family in Jacksonville, Florida, we made it a point to always visit the Naval Station in Mayport, Florida where I was stationed when I was on active duty. Back in the day when visitors were welcome aboard ship (before 9/11), we were able to freely tour the ships. See the photo below of Nicholas, Timothy, and me with my cousin Ben and three of his children, Shawn, Madeleine, and Christina, on the flight deck of the USS *Forrestal* (CVA-59).

Cousins aboard the USS *Forrestal* in Mayport, Florida.

One time we had the opportunity to tour aboard the HMS *Bristol*, a super-sized British destroyer docked there. I recall that one of the gun mounts on the *Bristol* had been removed and flooded with water to make a small pool for the sailors to swim in. With the after-mount removed, the crew would have to make do with one less gun should the need arise. Unlike U.S. Navy ships, I was surprised to learn that British sailors were allowed to have beer in their living quarters.

In addition to the ships we visited, I took the kids to the beach, the base bowling alley and pool. We often climbed the jetty that extended quite far out from the shoreline. We were cautious to monitor the tide; if the tide was coming in, we could have been stranded on the rocks far from shore. We had to know something about the tides.

Fishing in a Stocked Pond

On one of these outings to Mayport Naval Station, I took the "cousins"—Chris, Nicholas, Tim and all the Ossi cousins fishing at a stocked pond. The fish they caught could be purchased by the pound. The older kids started fishing first. By the time I had helped Timothy get his rod and hook squared away, the older ones were already landing their second and third fish. It was easy for them and I could see this was going to be the mother lode of fish for me to buy by the pound. I acted quickly, and in a loud voice, I said, "Stop fishing"—what a surprise for the kids! We were finished so fast, but we had a good time and a lot of fish to bring home. Some of the fish went back into the pond.

My boys were always interested in hearing my naval sea stories. They listened attentively. However, they never seemed enticed enough to express an intent to join the service. And as they grew up, it seemed that they never would. This was OK with me because over time, each one has launched himself on his own successful trajectory in life. Chris and Nicholas became medical doctors and Timothy studied music in Europe, majored in music education in college and has now become a music teacher. Each son has a wonderful wife and family—I have nine grandchildren in all.

Lake Juneau Safari Resort.

In their own special way, each of my sons has honored me as their father. For my 70th birthday, Chris and his wife Ann rented a place in a nature preserve stocked with more than 500 rare animals imported from Africa. Many of the animals were familiar, such as the zebras and giraffes. They seemed to cluster in pairs with others of their own type. We saw them up close and, also from an observation car pulled by a tractor. I could not distinguish what I was seeing from what I might experience on a safari in Africa.

Ricky, the giraffe.

Adele and Elise holding two of the smaller animals.

Thanksgiving in Lafayette, Louisiana

Chris and Ann gather the clan every Thanksgiving at their home in Lafayette, Louisiana. Chris once organized an outing for our large group. We paddled canoes down the Bayou Tesché. I could see that granddaughter Elise really enjoyed the water and eventually she asked me to tell her stories about my time in the Navy.

Chris and Nicholas on the Bayou Tesche

She had heard Navy stories from Charlie, her grandfather on Ann's side of the family (also a Navy Reservist) who worked with the Blue Angels promoting their air shows. Elise was testing the water to see whether a military career might be right for her.

In Private Practice

My son Chris is in private practice in Lafayette as an ear, nose and throat surgeon where he has dedicated his life to healing "one patient at a time." He is well-equipped as he graduated first in his medical school class at LSU New Orleans. His residency at Tulane was for 5 years and he would have done a 2-year fellowship after that to specialize in the ear except, after all that schooling, he was ready to start a family with Ann Marie. It was time to join a practice. Chris and I have enjoyed traveling together, to Alaska and to Oregon. On the Alaska trip there continues to be some contention as to whether we encountered a bear or not. Without a doubt, we encountered the roar of a bear on a trail that bears are known to frequent. Hearing this roar, we definitely didn't need to take a vote to decide to make a quick U-turn and walk the other way.

The Center for Disease Control and Prevention

When Nicholas completed medical school and his residency, he matched with the Center for Disease Control in Atlanta for a job in the Public Health Service as an epidemiologist. As a Public Health Officer, he chose to be in the Uniformed Corps. I was delighted. They gave him credit for his years of medical study which brought him in at a higher pay grade. He is based in Atlanta and has been deployed to developing countries all over the world. He even went to Africa (Guinea, Bissau) to fight the Ebola epidemic after living and serving elsewhere in Africa for four years with his family. He and his family (Adriana from Colombia, and children Nicole and Julian) love traveling and spending time in third world countries. They have traveled all over the world.

Travel to Lesotho in South Africa

In fact, I was fortunate to visit Nicholas and his family when they were in Lesotho in 2013, and happened to be there on the day that Nelson Mandela died. Adriana is a tireless planner and kept me busy every day I was there. On one trip to the Orange Free State in South Africa we stopped at a game preserve called Templehof. The photo below is of me holding a lion cub. Notice how our guide, Chris on the left, is keeping an eye on the other lion cub behind him.

Here, I'm holding a lion cub at the Templehof Nature Preserve.

In July 2018, Nicholas was selected for promotion to the rank of Captain (O-6 in the Public Health Service). A few months prior to the ceremony he asked me to do the honors and pin another stripe on his shoulder board at his promotion ceremony. I thought, "What an achievement for him and an honor for me." He was making O-6, a pretty high rank, and I would not have missed it for anything. Then he asked me to be there in uniform—summer whites. Could I find them and could I get into them all these years later?

Dad pins a stripe on Nicholas at his promotion ceremony in Atlanta.

That was the uniform I wore when I was on active duty, when I went to Vietnam, and when I served 23 years in the Naval Reserves. The Uniformed Corps of the Public Health Service wears the same uniform as the Navy except for some of the trimmings. The ceremony was held in Atlanta at the headquarters of the Center for Disease Control.

Putting on My Uniform One More Time

Most of my uniform was discarded long ago. I called the Uniform Support Center, and they verified my military standing (retired) and shipped me a new uniform via FedEx. I replaced my ribbons at the Marine Corps Exchange at Parris Island.

On the day of the ceremony, Nicholas and I both underwent a uniform check beforehand. We looked pretty good and we were ready. Wives and parents were in the audience. The admiral gave a stirring call to action directed to each promoted officer. We listened and responded with our own private feelings of patriotism. We all had a sense of the mission of the Public Health Service, and that is to save lives.

A music career for Timothy

When Timothy enrolled in college at Loyola University, New Orleans, he won a full scholarship for the entire 5-year program in music education. And because of the scholarship, his finances were in great shape when he graduated which allowed him to study for a year in Germany. He stayed with a family, learned German, performed with a university orchestra in Munich and had a complete cultural experience. He even looked up some "Gaffga" relatives and visited with them during that period. He was a leader in his class and maintained contact with the dean of the music school who helped place him in a teaching job in Les Vegas after his German experience. Tim eventually settled in Lafayette, met Lorna and they were married in 2013. Along with Maddie, Lorna's daughter, Tim and Lorna now have three more children between them: Lydia, Abigail, and Liam. Tim is pursuing his passion, teaching music (strings) in the public-school system and Lorna is a nurse in the neonatal ICU.

Tim is also a member of three regional orchestras: Rapides Symphony Orchestra based in Alexandria, Louisiana, the Lake Charles Symphony Orchestra now performing in its 60th season, and the Acadiana Symphony Orchestra which he will direct as honored clinician, a position he won by tryouts.

I am very proud of the next generation. The three boys are married, productive members of society, each with their own family—seven granddaughters and two grandsons. The grandchildren range in age from 18 to 2 years old. Nicole is now (fall 2019) a freshman at the University of Georgia. She interested in studying pre-med.

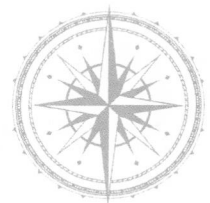

BIBLIOGRAPHY

Beardsley Charles, *Guam—Past and Present*, 1964.

Follet, Ken, *Fall of Giants*, 2010.

Freeman, Gregory A, *Sailors to the End—The Deadly Fire on the USS Forrestal and the Heroes Who Fought It*, 2004.

Mahon, Alfred T, *The Influence of Sea Power upon History*, 1890.

Nader, Ralph, *Unsafe at Any Speed*, 1965.

Riesenberg, Felix, *Bob Graham at Sea*, 1925.

Spear, E. Jon, *Navy Days: Memoirs of a Sailor in the 1960s*, 2010.

Toll, Ian W, *Pacific Crucible: War at Sea in the Pacific, 1941–1942*, 2011.

Toll, Ian W, *Six Frigates: The Epic History of the Founding of the U.S. Navy*, 2008.

Winchester, Simon, *Krakatoa: The Day the World Exploded: August 27, 1883*, 2005.

ABOUT THE WRITER/
ADVENTURER

Lieutenant Commander Gaffga is now retired from IBM and from the Naval Reserves and lives in Sun City, Hilton Head, South Carolina. He was born in New York City and moved to Garden City, Long Island with his family when he was 9 years old. He graduated from Garden City High School in 1960 and was accepted at Yale University where he graduated in 1964 with a BA degree in economics. After completing 4 years of active naval service as a reservist, he graduated from the Wharton Business School with an MBA in 1970 and was recruited by IBM. He has been teaching at the university level since retiring from IBM. He last taught international economy (global economics) as an Adjunct (2006–2014) at the University of South Carolina Beaufort.